REDISCOVE...
TURTLE ISLAND

"The official history of the United States begins with Spanish contact in the late fifteenth century. The oral traditions and legends of the various Native peoples of North America, however, stretch back much earlier, into the opaque mists of preliterate times. With a member of the Earthen Bison Clan of the Omaha Tribe to serve as our guide, *Rediscovering Turtle Island* leads the reader along near-forgotten, overgrown paths that twist and turn throughout a resacralized landscape, decorated with ancient landmarks, populated with whispering ghosts and supernatural beings. The sacred geography of America will never again appear the same."

P. D. NEWMAN, AUTHOR OF *NATIVE AMERICAN SHAMANISM AND THE AFTERLIFE JOURNEY IN THE MISSISSIPPI VALLEY*

"Taylor Keene has written a fascinating story of North America that integrates scholarship and mythology in a very entertaining and readable way. His linkage of some of the North American creation stories to the places where they are told and their representations in carvings and drawings is fascinating. He interweaves aspects of North America's history, cosmology, and geography from an Indigenous perspective, which, combined with the sharing of his own life experience, uplifts us and demonstrates how we are all related."

LEWIS MEHL-MADRONA, M.D., PH.D., AUTHOR OF *NARRATIVE MEDICINE*, *REMAPPING YOUR MIND*, AND *COYOTE WISDOM*

"What could be more fascinating than the origin of mankind itself? The premise is staggering and the consequences far-reaching. Keen's hard work pays off immensely in *Rediscovering Turtle Island*, and readers will be gripped by that experience on every page."

SIDIAN M.S. JONES, COAUTHOR OF *THE VOICE OF ROLLING THUNDER*

REDISCOVERING
TURTLE ISLAND

A First Peoples' Account of the Sacred Geography of America

A Sacred Planet Book

TAYLOR KEEN

Bear & Company
Rochester, Vermont

Bear & Company
One Park Street
Rochester, Vermont 05767
www.BearandCompanyBooks.com

Text stock is SFI certified

Bear & Company is a division of Inner Traditions International

Sacred Planet Books are curated by Richard Grossinger, Inner Traditions editorial board member and cofounder and former publisher of North Atlantic Books. The Sacred Planet collection, published under the umbrella of the Inner Traditions family of imprints, includes works on the themes of consciousness, cosmology, alternative medicine, dreams, climate, permaculture, alchemy, shamanic studies, oracles, astrology, crystals, hyperobjects, locutions, and subtle bodies.

Copyright © 2024 by Taylor Keen

Cataloging-in-Publication Data for this title is available from the Library of Congress

ISBN 978-1-59143-520-4 (print)
ISBN 978-1-59143-521-1 (ebook)

Printed and bound in the United States by Lake Book Manufacturing, LLC
The text stock is SFI certified. The Sustainable Forestry Initiative® program promotes sustainable forest management.

10 9 8 7 6 5 4 3 2 1

Text design by Virginia Scott Bowman and layout by Debbie Glogover
This book was typeset in Garamond Premier Pro with Brioso Pro, Gothiks Condensed, Gill Sans MT Pro, ITC Legacy Sans, and Myriad Pro used as display typefaces

To send correspondence to the author of this book, mail a first-class letter to the author c/o Inner Traditions • Bear & Company, One Park Street, Rochester, VT 05767, and we will forward the communication, or contact the author directly at **rediscoveringturtleisland.com**.

Scan the QR code and save 25% at InnerTraditions.com. Browse over 2,000 titles on spirituality, the occult, ancient mysteries, new science, holistic health, and natural medicine.

CONTENTS

FOREWORD

CHARLES C. MANN

The book you are holding in your hands is special, as is its author, Taylor Keen. I'm going to explain why I think this, but to do that I'll first need to muddle around a bit, like a dog circling around before finding its place on the carpet.

About fifteen years ago, I went to Xinjiang, in far northwestern China, on a research trip. I was writing a book that was partly about the consequences of trade across the Pacific, which began in the 1560s, soon after Spain conquered the Philippines. Xinjiang had felt many of those consequences, and I was there to try to learn from local scholars a little about what had happened.

Harsh, dry, and ringed by mountains, Xinjiang was often eerily beautiful. It was one of the most remote places I'd ever been. In villages, I was (understandably) an object of curiosity. Kids followed me around. Twice, local officials asked if they could take selfies with me.

A few days of traveling about made it obvious that this region was different from the rest of China, and that difference had a lot to do with its history. Northern Xinjiang was originally inhabited by Uyghur people (Turkic-speaking Muslim farmers, who mostly lived around oases). Southern Xinjiang's first peoples were Dzungar, nomadic Tibetan Buddhists. Both had fought for centuries to keep their culture intact against waves of foreign invaders, most of them from eastern China.

Wanting to learn more about this, I found a bookstore with several histories of the region, originally written in Chinese but translated into English, all inexpensive paperbacks. I bought the books and began looking through them.

To my surprise, all were written from the point of view of the invaders from eastern China. After a few cursory pages about the millennia-long history of Xinjiang, the books skipped to the seventeenth-century Qing Dynasty, which began China's serious efforts to take over the area. After that, the histories recounted how Xinjiang had finally become part of China. The Uyghur and Dzungar peoples were described as, variously, "brave," "savage," and "primitive," but the implicit view was that they were fated to disappear and become good citizens of modern China, indistinguishable from all the others. Their version of the story—or even the idea that they might *have* their own version of the story—wasn't a factor.

A little bit later, the penny dropped.

About 400 years ago, my ancestors joined the horde of Europeans who were invading Turtle Island (the name many of North America's first peoples use for their home). They came to a place that was a thriving tumult of cultures, languages, beliefs, and ways of life. There were more religions than all of Asia, more language families in what is now California than all of Europe, and an incredible variety of cuisines. There were desert peoples, forest peoples, peoples of the plains and mountains and shorelines—a crazy-quilt jumble of different ways to be human.

My ancestors and the other newcomers built a new nation and a new culture here. But they did that by suppressing all those hundreds of other nations and cultures. Or, at any rate, they *tried* to suppress them.

Like all people, my ancestors told stories about themselves, and how they got where they were. They wrote histories of the United States, of North America, and the Americas as a whole. That history formed the backdrop of countless novels, movies, poems, and songs. In all of those stories, my ancestors put themselves in the starring role, and told the stories in their own voices.

Nothing in itself is wrong with that. In fact, though, most of those other nations, societies, and cultures—the first peoples of Turtle Island—survived. They came through everything my ancestors could throw at them and are still standing. And so there's been a yawning gap. The real Turtle Island—the real North America—is a chorus of voices. But a huge number of those voices have gone unheard. One reason why is that for a very long time the chronicles—the histories, the novels, the movies, the epic poems and songs—were almost all written by people like me (in fact, by me personally—I wrote one of those histories). Even when Native people did tell their tales in first person, it was almost always *through* a non-Native scholar, writer, or editor.

That is beginning to change. The book in your hands is evidence of that. It is, I believe, just one of the first droplets in what will be a river of stories from cultures all over this beautiful country we share. Over time, those previously overlooked voices will change the way everyone here thinks about their past, confronts the present, and faces the future.

It's hard for me to imagine anyone better equipped to be at the front of this new movement than Taylor Keen.

Taylor Keen is *a lot*.

A member of the Omaha Tribe and an enrolled Cherokee citizen, he grew up in both nations and has a name from each—"Bison Mane," from his mother's people, the Omaha, in Nebraska; "Blackberry," from his father's people, the Cherokee, in Oklahoma. (I am, of course, giving the English translation of both names.) His mother, Octa, a nurse, was directly descended from the legendary Omaha chief Big Elk. His father, Ralph, was chief justice of the Cherokee Supreme Court, then called the Judicial Appeals Tribunal.

Taylor lived up to his distinguished lineage. As a student, he was a standout as much on the Rugby pitch as in the classroom. He got his undergraduate degree at Dartmouth College and went to work for Bath Iron Works, a shipbuilding firm in Maine. Encouraged by a mentor, the Cherokee leader Wilma Mankiller, he applied to Harvard as a joint-degree candidate at the Kennedy School of Government and Harvard Business School. He was accepted but deferred his admission to work with the Omaha on reinvesting their gaming profits into housing and small loans to tribal members' businesses. Once at Harvard, he picked up two master's degrees—one in public policy, and an MBA—all the while serving as a Fellow in the Harvard Project on American Indian Economic Development.

After graduating, he worked for Worldcom, where he helped build the first fully redundant, transatlantic, fiber-optic communications network. The project was successful, his colleagues enjoyable, and the paycheck substantial, but after two years he realized that it was not where his heart lay. He returned to Oklahoma, where he served as vice president of Cherokee Enterprises, the nation's business arm, and a tribal councilor.

Anyone who has been around Indigenous politics knows how tumultuous it can be. In 2007, Taylor got tired of the dust-ups and moved to Omaha, where he founded his own consulting firm. At the same time, he joined the faculty of Creighton University's College of Business Administration and, later, became board chairman of the Blackbird Bend Corporation, the Omaha Nation's gaming operation, where he helped put the nation's two casinos on firm footing.

That's a lot of verbiage.* Maybe the simplest way to put it is that

---

*And I haven't mentioned his stints as a trustee of the Nebraska State Historical Society and board member of Humanities Nebraska. Oh, and he was a Golden Gloves boxer. Like I said, Taylor is *a lot*.

Taylor is somebody who stands easily in many worlds. The world of today, with its giant economic enterprises and burgeoning technology. The world of the future, teaching kids, Native and newcomer alike, how to make their way. The world of the past, with its timeless values.

An important voice for today. A storyteller's voice.

While he was working for the Omaha, Taylor founded Sacred Seed—which is how I came to meet him. Sacred Seed is a nonprofit that preserves Native American heritage by collecting, growing, and disseminating the seeds of maize (corn) and other traditional Indigenous foods. I met him one hot summer morning in one of Sacred Seed's gardens. That day, he had protected himself against the sun with a moisture-wicking shirt and a red, white, and blue baseball cap. Around his neck hung a shell gorget: a mother-of-pearl disc with an eagle-and-wolf design styled after Keen's Cherokee ancestors.

The Sacred Seed plot was in downtown Omaha, not far from the freeway. To my eye, the area looked like any rundown neighborhood that had been strafed by urban renewal. The forces of gentrification had set up their familiar redoubts: a hip deli, a natural-therapy center, a condo complex with postmodern filigree, and, of course, an art gallery. Across the street from a dead gas station was Keen's cornfield.

Purple-and-white Cherokee maize grew on two low mounds, mixed with other crops: black Trail of Tears beans (another Cherokee variety), Lakota squash (compact, orange), and Mongolian giant sunflower (an Asian version of this American plant, which Keen chose because its immense height amused him). Omaha tradition refers to these species as the Four Sisters. Another mound housed different variants of the sisters—Arikara sunflower, for instance. Smaller mounds featured flowering plants (milkweed, tobacco) and prairie species (little bluestem, Indian plantain). Paths cut through the garden in an artful manner that suggested attention from the gallery nearby.

The maize had already tasseled out, fifteen to twenty long spikes rising from the top of every plant. From the spikes emerged tiny green packets that looked a bit like seeds. As the plant matured, the packets opened. Out dropped two purple cylinders, each about the size of a rice grain, dangling from the packets on thin white stems like airplane oxygen masks. When conditions were right, the cylinders opened and released puffs of purple pollen.

Softly murmuring old Peyote music songs, Keen took some of the pollen cylinders from one plant and sprinkled their contents over the silk on other plants. When a mote of pollen touched a threadlike silk, the silk would develop a thin, interior tunnel—a pollen tube—that traveled down the silk and carried the genetic material from the pollen to the ovary at the bottom of the silk. After pollination, each thread of silk would create one maize kernel.

In about 2009, not long after his arrival in Omaha, Taylor told me, he was called by a friend, Deward Walker, a retired anthropologist at the University of Colorado. "He said, 'Young man, what are you doing to protect your corn?' I said, 'Do what?' And he told me—begged me—to stop our corn from disappearing." Industrial agriculture, which prizes uniformity, was effectively wiping out most maize varieties, including those from Native peoples. Walker told Taylor he should ensure their survival. Taylor was struck by his urgency, but he had never farmed and didn't know how to do what Walker wanted.

Despite his lack of experience with the hoe, events in his life kept nudging him toward picking it up. He learned that Cherokee people in Oklahoma were bringing back their traditional maize. He began looking for Omaha seeds: squash seeds, bean seeds, maize seeds. In 2016 he was asked to identify some old Omaha artifacts at the Buffalo Bill Center of the West, in Cody, Wyoming. He was nervous about the responsibility, he said, and as the trip to Cody approached he prayed for strength.

Among the artifacts at the museum was a plastic bag, sealed in old yellowed packing tape. He slowly lifted the tape with his knife. Inside was a century-old ear of maize, husk still intact. It had been mounted on a stick. Four blue lines had been painted down its sides. Maize, a product of sun and earth, was a symbol of the protective Mother. This painted object had been used to bless newborn children. The U.S. government had suppressed Indigenous religions and their artifacts, formally banning most of them in 1883. Nothing like this painted maize had been seen for more than 100 years.

"I felt a shock," Taylor told me. "I was being told to grow my corn—this corn." It was a message he was at last ready to hear. Sacred Seed's maize, he said, "isn't for the market." He said, "I don't sell it. I don't object to markets but this is for something else." His name in Omaha is Ba'gee-zha (referring, as I mentioned, to the fur ruff on a bison's head and neck). With a smile, he showed me his hands, stained purple by Cherokee pollen. "This is for Ba'gee-zha," he said.

Sacred Seed came into existence at about the same time as dozens of other programs to bring back customary forms of food and agriculture. Indigenous seed banks in the Northeast and Southwest, tribal-run fishing grounds on the West Coast, Native agricultural programs in the Southeast—all, like Sacred Seed, are efforts to restore traditional practices in a context that fits the time we are living in.

Taylor, too, has spread his seeds. Some are now growing in the Land Institute, in Kansas, where researchers are trying to learn more about their properties. Another garden is rising at the Tri-Faith Partnership, a Christian-Jewish-Muslim initiative that, with Taylor, is welcoming another spiritual tradition. And still another is at a collaboration with the University of Kansas and the Omaha Tribal Language Program. I have no doubt that by the time you read this Taylor will have found more partners.

This book is like those seeds. It is something informed by the past to be used in the present to build the future. It is for everyone by a very particular someone from a tradition that has all too often gone unheard.

It is something from an ancient country that fits into a modern city. It is among the first of many efforts, and it will spread.

Like a puff of purple pollen wafting in the breeze, this book is like nothing most people have ever seen before while being something they will instantly want to know more about.

I hope—I believe—you will get as much pleasure from hearing Taylor's story in this book as I have learning from him in his cornfield.

A correspondent for *The Atlantic, Science,* and *Wired,* CHARLES C. MANN is the author of *1491,* winner of the National Academies of Science Keck Award for best book of the year; *1493,* a New York Times best-seller; and, most recently, *The Wizard and the Prophet* as well as the coauthor of *Noah's Choice* and *The Second Creation.* His next book, a history of the North American West, will be published by Knopf in 2025. He lives in Massachusetts.

PREFACE

The genesis of this written work began in the early 2000s with the consecutive births of four albino bison, signaling the beginning of the Indigenous prophecy of the Seventh Generation. This prophecy not only ended six previous generations of suffering for Indigenous peoples but was also the genesis of hope; the Seventh Generation of Indigenous peoples would lead tribal nations to stand tall and shepherd in a transformational cultural resurgence. I honor this prophecy through my work and can testify that today an Indigenous cultural resurgence is occurring with tribal language preservation, restoration of Plant and Animal Nation lifeways, sacred geography protection (such as the UNESCO designation of the Hopewell Ceremonial Works), and the desire of First Peoples to represent their own history and to strive to be economically self-reliant. Equally as important, the prophecy of Seventh Generation teaches that non-Indigenous children born after the fourth albino bison would also be the generation that would finally be receptive to the cultural teachings of Indigenous peoples. Together, I believe, we can find solutions for Mother Earth that benefit the planet and our mutual humanity.

This book is the focal point for my attempt as a sixth-generation Indigenous teacher to impart as much knowledge as I can for the seventh generation. I sought to answer some of the most human questions:

Where do First Peoples come from? What should we be aspiring to do?

With the passing of the Lakota thought leader Vine Deloria Jr. in the fall of 2005, I lamented the fact that his written works, such as *Custer Died for your Sins, God Is Red,* and *The World We Used to Live In,* would not continue. An Osage friend and legal scholar, Elizabeth Homer, challenged me to pick up where Vine Deloria left off and write something that would continue the tradition. After much self-denial, I realized that this would be a tremendously difficult endeavor, but that if I emerged on the other side, I would be better for it, and I might make a meaningful contribution to society.

Another lifelong friend and mentor, Deward Walker, PhD, chair emeritus of anthropology at the University of Colorado Boulder introduced me many years ago to the study of sacred tribal geography as well as the importance of tribal seed stewardship This led to my founding of SacredSeed.Org, which is dedicated to educating others on the importance of Indigenous agricultural lifeways.

I want to acknowledge Dr. William F. Romain, archaeologist, archaeoastronomer, author, and friend, for all his advice and constructive criticism in the preparation of this manuscript. Bill's academic advice was invaluable, but his honest feedback as a mentor to me as an Indigenous first-time author meant even more to me. *WibthaHo, wado,* and thank you, Dr. Romain.

This work would not have found a publishing home with Inner Traditions without the vision and wisdom from Richard Grossinger. Richard believed in the work and in myself, and has helped at every step of this work, which is paramount for a first-time author. Many thanks to my project editor, Renée Heitman, copy editor Lesley Allen, Editor in Chief Jeanie Levitan, and all of the staff at Inner Traditions.

My intention with the book was to make something impactful, yet beautiful to the reader. The "heart" of the book was the chapter on Cahokia, where the muse inspired me to share the story of the rise and fall of the Cahokian Empire through the eyes of someone who would become a powerful dynastic leader in that era. I named him Honga, which is a powerful, ancient, and mysterious word for the Omaha people. I believe the name Honga represents the name of an ancient, larger tribe, from whom many Siouan-speaking tribes are descended. This notion embodies the tribal core value of "We are all related."

The mysteries of the Mound Builder era illustrate the complexity and depth of ancient Indigenous peoples. To those voices that decried Indigenous peoples as illiterate savages, I respond with evidence in the ancient earthen works, advanced applied mathematics, complex civil engineering and construction techniques, Indigenous urban cities, and far-ranging economic trading empires. We find an Indigenous civilization as profound and ancient as other great societies, such as the Egyptian and Sumerian civilizations.

Recent discoveries such as the Louisiana State University Campus Mounds yield carbon dating back to 11,000 years ago, and fossilized footprints in White Sands, New Mexico, have been carbon-dated to between 21,000 and 23,000 years ago. This changes the entire narrative regarding the true provenance of the antiquity of Indigenous peoples on Turtle Island. While there are critics who challenge these facts, the timeline of the antiquity of Indigenous peoples will only get pushed back further in time. How and when did Indigenous peoples arrive here in what we call the Americas today? I hope to further explore this topic in future editions of this work.

But more important is the beauty of what ancient Indigenous peoples accomplished: a complex archaeoastronomy of earthen works to reflect the heavens above, the Journey of the Souls and a Principia Theologica, a true Indigenous esoteric tradition tied to the original truths of a central humanity found in ancient wisdom across the world. It is my hope that the beauty embodied in the ancient Indigenous past will inspire the next seven generations to continue to forge a legacy that inspires people of the world to love the Earth as their own mother: rediscovering Turtle Island and all her beautiful esoteric mysteries.

A Note to the Reader about the Artwork

While the research for this work involved the study of many Indigenous articles of antiquity, I have been very careful to not include any images that would be considered unsuitable for publication by most Indigenous peoples. I have tried to follow the spirit of the intent of the Native American Graves Protection and Repatriation Act (NAGPRA) so as not to include any ancestral remains, funerary objects, sacred objects, or objects of cultural patrimony that are directly attributable to any federally recognized tribe. However, there are a few images of some petroglyphs/rock art and carved figurines (not from burial mounds) that are not attributable to any one tribe today and are indicative of a collective history of Indigenous peoples. I felt strongly that education around these topics would outweigh any offense taken by those who disagree with me.

COSMOGENESIS

The Earth Diver Mythos,
an Ancient Creation Cosmology

*It has always been the prime function of mythology and rite
to supply the symbols that carry the human spirit forward,
in counteraction to those that tend to tie it back. . . . If we
could dredge up something forgotten not only by ourselves
but by our whole generation or our entire civilization, we
should become indeed the boon-bringer, the culture hero of
the day—a personage of not only local but world historical
moment.*

JOSEPH CAMPBELL,
THE HERO WITH A THOUSAND FACES

Stories, parables, and myths are forever enduring and are perhaps a lineage that can be traced and compared to tie different cultures together cosmologically and illustrate how cultures are related through story.

The Earth Diver Myth, often referred to as the Diving Bird Myth, is a common oral tradition across many of the tribes of North America. From Algonquian, Athabascan, and Siouan speakers, there are variations of this story, with various creatures being the conduit for the Great Spirit as the successful diver into primordial waters to bring up the clay that shall become the earthen continents.

The following version is a Dhegihan-Sioux derivation that is central to the Omaha, Ponca, Osage, Quapaw, and Kaw tribes. I heard a version of this story much earlier in my life, and it always resonated, like a connection to me from my ancient past.

In the Beginning, our souls were like stars in the sky—thought, but no form. The Teachings tell us that our souls come from the Seven Sisters constellation, and eventually that is to which we will return. There came a point in time that one of those souls asked the question, "Who am I?" And that question burned like a brilliant fire within the young star, so he went to his mother, the Moon, and asked, "Mother, who am I?"

"Oh, my child, now that you have asked that question, everything must change." And she was sad, as if she knew what must happen next. "Hurry, go tell your father what you have told me."

And so that star went to his father, the Sun, and asked him, "Father, who am I?"

And his father answered, "Now that you have asked that question, everything must change." With caution, he added, "Be careful with that question, for that is the most important question we have, as souls."

But that star was like we are today. We can't keep a secret very well, especially a good secret, and soon there were four souls who asked that same question. The People Who Move Against the Current know that the teachings say that everything happens in fours, especially the Journey of the Souls. And so, these first four souls began their journey from our true home, the Seven Sisters, and they went through the center of the Spiral, the Milky Way, and were guided by the Morning Star to our temporal home, the mother.

But when they landed on Earth, they found that their new home was covered in water and that they had taken on new forms, two males and two females, a Turtle and a Waterfowl, and an Otter and a Deer.

It was the Turtle who had first asked the question, "Who am I?" and he took notice of the form the Creator had given him. He noticed that his shell was solid, and he could easily float on the water or dive deep, and his paws were made easily for the water, webbed, yet maybe they were meant for something else, too.

The Waterfowl took notice of his body and noticed that he floated on the water and his feet were webbed, but he had powerful wings, and he might be able to float in the air much like he did in the water.

The Otter took notice of her form and that she, too, had webbed paws and her coat of fur was glorious and sleek, and she, too was made for the water, with her powerful tail, but perhaps she, too, was made for something different.

Finally, the Deer took notice of her form and that she, unlike the others, was not meant for the water. Her body did not float well, and her hooves were made for something else. She became afraid as she struggled to stay afloat.

The Turtle felt bad, as he felt responsible for their journey together, and he remembered the Teachings, "Help one another. Be kind to one another. We are all related." And so he said he would dive deep to see what he could find, and he asked the Waterfowl to take to the air, flying larger and larger circles over and away from their emergence point. And so they went, and the Otter stayed to help her sister, the Deer, who struggled to stay afloat.

After much time had passed, they saw the Waterfowl flying in to land and the Turtle rising through the waters deep, and both were despondent as they said they found nothing.

The Otter said, "Let me go look, brother, my tail is strong, let me find something to help sister Deer."

So Otter went into the deep, dark, and cold water. Turtle lifted the Deer from below, and the Waterfowl grabbed her by the neck and lifted from above. Though Deer was struggling, the others encouraged her to live.

Just when all hope seemed lost, and they all began to feel weak, they saw a dark form, undulating from the depths, and saw that Otter was holding something in her paws, close to her chest, and knew it must be something very precious. She showed the Clay to them, and they knew it was a sacred gift from the Creator.

Turtle knew then what he must do, as he felt responsible for all of them on their journey. He took the Clay and placed it on his back, and the Earth formed out of his back. To this day, we call this place, Turtle Island and Mother Earth, our home.

It is out of respect for Turtle Island and Mother Earth that when we sing with our sacred drums, we always remember her heartbeat, for as long as we sing and beat our sacred drums, so will her heart keep on beating.

I have decided to explore the true origins of the Earth Diver Myth (EDM), so that I might be able to connect this story with other cultures to see where Indigenous peoples of the Americas originally came from.

The scholar Vladimir Napolskikh, in his research of the many variations of the Earth Diver Myth, suggests "an ethnohistorical interpretation of the spread in Northern Eurasia and North America of the myth of creation of the Earth from a small piece of soil brought up from the bottom of the primordial ocean by a therio-, anthropo or theomorphic diver. . . . It was demonstrated that this motif had a very ancient (at least upper Paleolithic) origin in Northern Asia . . . but the idea of success among several divers of the last one possessing not a physical, but a special supernatural power. The motifs close to this type are widely spread in North America."[1]

I am not arguing that Indigenous peoples did not cross the Bering Strait. I am arguing that cosmological and DNA research points out the many ways that all human beings are tied to each other or that "we are all related," as you hear in so many tribal core values in North America.

From an Indigenous perspective, our stories are our most powerful tools to convey wisdom, and to find the commonalities of these creation stories dispersed across so wide a geographical reach is mind-boggling. To wonder about how old the EDM is, and its true antiquity is beyond comprehension.

Napolskikh also explores the role of the mythical Upper and Lower Realms associated with this EDM, and it appears as an important part of the cosmologies of many global cultures. This "world-view system was suggested to have been present in the culture of the Proto-Uralic speakers living till the 6ᵗʰ–4ᵗʰ mil. BC in the Taiga Forest of Western Siberia and the Urals." Regardless of when certain tribal people left the areas in Siberia to migrate to what would become America, the antiquity of these stories has a provenance to meet most theories on when exactly that migration occurred.

THE TREE OF LIFE, THE UPPER AND LOWER REALMS, AND THE ANCIENT COSMOLOGY OF AMERICA

From this beautiful creation story and the associated cosmology with an age gone by, now rediscovered at the Mississippian-era site known as Picture Cave, comes the sacred site where the ancestors of the Osage, Omaha, Ponca, Quapaw, and Kaw resided around 1000 CE on the outskirts of the Cahokian Empire, the Womb of the Universe.[2]

I had heard of this site over the past ten years, but for some unknown reason, it was shrouded in secrecy. I heard rumors that select elders had seen it. Finally, in 2015 a book was published entitled *Picture Cave: Unraveling the Mysteries of the Mississippian Cosmos,* which revealed many of her mysteries.

Situated somewhere within a hundred miles of the ceremonial urban center of Cahokia, Picture Cave appears to have been one of the satellite communities in Cahokia's orbit. Dotted with petroglyphs of black and red, the images tell a story of a cosmology influenced by the Cahokian Empire.

One of the elders who visited the cave, Osage artist Anita Fields, who is a longtime family friend, said of her experience of visiting Picture Cave: "I am familiar with the earth. The earth holds me up; it sustains me and provides for the needs and nourishment of my children. I understand that the layers of the earth contain the mysteries of the past and hold our collective history."

> The visit to Picture Cave was an experience that left me with mixed emotions, some profoundly deep, some conflicting, questioning, and felt with a degree of sadness. Beneath the floor of the forest, layers of rock, and folds of the earth, I descended into the dark, cool, damp cavity of the earth. In front, on all sides and beneath a rock shelf below me the memory of the earth was revealed. Within the powerful presence of nature, evidence of early Indigenous culture was exposed through an extraordinary series of marks, symbols, representations, and color.[3]

The images of the petroglyphs of Picture Cave are at once primeval and haunting, and they have their own story to tell, a story once widely heard across the land that would soon become the United States of America.

> *A long time ago, after the beginning, there was a time when we Human Beings could speak to the Animals, and the world was young.*
>
> *We are from the Stars, born of the cosmic dust, winds, light, and darkness. In the Beginning, our souls were like stars in the sky; thought but no form.*
>
> *Before us, came First Man and First Woman, who are the children of the Sun (father) and the Moon (mother). Both the first man and first woman have many other names: some call him Symbolic Man,*

others the Hunter; some call her Mother Corn, others the Woman Who Fell from the Sky.

At the Center of the Dhegihan Universe stood the great and ancient Tree of Life, in which lies the mysteries of our world, and of ourselves. It is said that in the branches of the Tree of Life are the Upper Realm of the known Universe, ruled by the Thunder Beings, whose messengers are the Thunderbirds, for their cry is thunder, and lightning comes from their eyes.

Below we have a *Wazhazhe* or Osage representation of the Tree of Life, made by J. Owen Dorsey in 1885 after interviewing Red Corn. At the vertical "top" we see the Tree of Life, a cedar sacred for its red interior and the aromatic qualities of its leaves. The Tree of Life stands next

Fig. 1.1. This is an illustration example of the Indigenous Tree of Life, the Axis Mundi.
J. Owen Dorsey, 1885

to a river, and just under the river is a large star representing the Red, or Morning, Star. Immediately to the right of the Morning Star are two clumps of stars, totaling six, and then in the center is the Evening Star, and then the Small Star. Below these four sets of stars are the seven sisters of the Pleiades, flanked on both sides by the Moon and the Sun. Beneath the Pleiades is a hatchet and a peace pipe. Beneath all the stars we see a bird over several arches, or perhaps a rainbow, and in this realm, there are three levels, the Upper, Middle, and Lower Realms supported by a large Oak Tree, whose roots run, oh, so very deep.[4]

We begin our study of these three realms with the Upper Realm. The Upper Realm is ruled by Thunderbirds, who are messengers of the Thunder Beings.

The Thunder Beings are the original Sky People, to whom we pay homage and who taught us some of their wisdom, so that we could survive, if not thrive, on this world, and they taught us that the Earth is our mother and that we must protect and live in harmony with the Plants and the Animals. This is the great Covenant.

To balance out the power of the Upper Realm, the Creator made the Lower Realm. One is not better than the other, for we need both for there to be harmony in the Universe.

The Lower Realm is in the roots of the Tree of Life and is ruled by the Underwater Serpent. The Underwater Serpent is said to reside underneath the Earth, living in the underwater springs, emerging from time to time from an earthen portal, a place of Emergence. The Underwater Serpent has a long spiraling tail that coils like the Milky Way, and it has great horns, and within these horns it holds a great crystal, the most powerful crystal in the world, and any medicine person who should steal it from the Underwater Serpent should be the most powerful medicine person in the world. There are many other lesser, minor Water Spirits in the Lower Realm, and they can be powerful.

Fig. 1.2a. This image is an example of the petroglyphs representing the Underwater Serpent or the Underwater Panther, from Picture Cave.
Image courtesy of Carol Diaz-Granados

Fig 1.2b. An illustration of art representing the Underwater Serpent or Underwater Panther.
Artwork courtesy of Isiah Stewart (Lakota/Mohawk)

There is a sacred tension between the Upper Realm and the Lower Realm. That tension, like yin and yang, must be balanced. If there is an imbalance, then there are repercussions. But like the good and evil in us all, there are tipping points, weaknesses, and fears.

First Man, sometimes called White Plume, for the large avian plume he symbolically wears in his hair, decides that he must journey to the Lower Realm to seek a battle with a Water Spirit, a powerful Beaver-tailed spirit, rumored to have eaten two Spirit Wolfs from the Upper Realm. A powerful battle ensues, and the Water Spirit is victorious over First Father and vanquishes him, keeping his head while allowing his body to return to the Upper Realm.

The Sun and the Moon are parents of six children, three males and three females; the oldest son is First Father, often called White Plume, who was vanquished in the Lower Realm.[5]

In some of the stories, a daughter of First Father and Mother Corn bears the Twins who will become the great warriors who journey to the Lower Realm to seek vengeance for their grandfather, First Father, and to return the head of First Father to his body so that he may be restored and experience the sacred rebirth after a symbolic death. In the Dhegihan cosmology, the names of the Twins are the Stone and the Gray Wolf.

The Twins are successful in avenging the death of First Father and return victorious to the Upper Realm, but the result of the intermingling of powers of both the Upper and Lower Realms creates an imbalance in the cosmos, and a void is created between the Upper and Lower Realm, and thus the Middle Realm, where we reside today, was created by Grandmother Spider as she spun and wove our Middle Realm.

Fig. 1.3a. Thunder Twins Battle a Water Spirit (Beaver). Picture Cave.
Image courtesy of Carol Diaz-Granados

Fig. 1.3b. Herb Roe's artistic interpretation, "Hero Twins" emerging from a crack in the back of a raccoon-faced Horned Serpent.
Wikimedia Commons

Fig. 1.4. Grandmother Spider, Weaver of the Middle Realms.
Image courtesy of Carol Diaz-Granados

REDHORN, THE TWINS AND THE MORNINGSTAR CONNECTION

And from there we have the stage set for what is the hallmark of the story: the raising of First Father by the Redhorn Trinity. Like the Father, Son, and Holy Ghost of Christianity, the myth of Redhorn in this story morphs from his own life as the youngest son to First Father, expressed in his progeny of the Twins, and then all three metamorphose into the celestial deity called Morningstar.

In this next pictograph we see the visages of Morningstar, with his deer antler headpiece with five arrows, his "long nose god" earrings, a bow in his left hand, and the severed head of White Plume (not the large plume to the right of his head). Morningstar is above White Plume's head, as if he were lifting it from the Lower Realm. To the right and slightly beneath Morningstar / Redhorn is an upside-down slain deer.

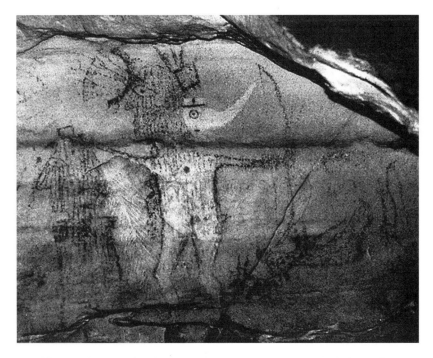

Fig. 1.5. Image of a thousand-year-old plus petroglyph from the
archaeological site of Picture Cave, representing the story of Redhorn
retrieving the severed head of the slain First Father / White Plume
to return it to the Upper Realm.
Image courtesy of Carol Diaz-Granados

We now come to the iconic panel often called the Redhorn Panel,
but there are many differing opinions about almost everything depicted
in the panel.

The term "Redhorn" comes from the present-day Ho-Chunk (mis-
takenly referred to as Winnebago), who has a "stellar" representation
in the stars. James Duncan, in his work with Carol Diaz-Granados,
"Of Masks and Myths" speculates that the central figure, Redhorn, or
"He-Who-Wears-Human-Head-Earrings," in Ho-Chunk lore, represents the Morning Star, or Venus, as the Morning Star precedes the Sun
on its rising in the horizon at pertinent times of the year.

While on the topic of Redhorn, or "Wears-Human-Head-Earrings,"
we have a variation in the stories, depending on the tribes, although the

tribes and the stories are related physically and figuratively. Paul Radin, who was an anthropologist and protégé of Franz Boaz, interviewed a Ho-Chunk elder by the name of Jasper Blowsnake who recounted the following oral tradition, which I take the artistic license of embellishing into a narrative form, but all based on the words of Blowsnake, as documented by Radin:

> *A long time ago, the Ho-Chunk people were still united with other related tribes, such as their brothers and sister tribes the Otoe and the Ioway, and their cousins the Dhegihan relatives: the Omaha, the Osage, the Ponca, the Quapaw, and the Kansa or Kaw.*
>
> *These were the days when the Upper Realm was ruled by sacred and powerful Thunderbirds, whose eyes could explode in lightning and whose piercing cry would roar like the Thunder, and the clouds would boil black with the strikes of electricity in the sky. These were the days when the Lower Realm was inhabited by underwater spirits and ruled by the Underwater Serpent or Panther.*
>
> *It was in these great days of old that a hero existed, the youngest of a group of brothers, whom they called "He-Who-Gets-Hit-With-Deer-Lungs." Being the youngest of these brothers, they often teased him, as brothers do, and sometimes threw things at him—such as the precious deer lungs, often a delicacy of their people—when they felt he disobeyed them. And on one occasion, he refused to eat the treasured delicacy, and the stories said that the brothers threw the lungs of the deer at him as a penance.*
>
> *It was then that the young brother revealed the truth to them. "Those in the heavens who created me did not call me by the name, He-Who-Gets-Hit-With-Deer-Lungs," he told them. "They called me, He-Who-Wears-Human-Heads-As-Earrings." And at that, he "spat upon his hands and began fingering his ears. And as he did this, little faces suddenly appeared on his ears, laughing, winking, and sticking out their tongues."*

And his magical powers did not end there; he spat upon his hands and rubbed it into his long hair, and it turned the color of red ocher, and he braided it into one single braid, or Horn. His powers also allowed him to turn himself into an arrow, which could speed faster than a man could run."[6]

A reminder that the Sun in this cosmogeneology is the primary male deity, or the father of First Man, and thus the original male ancestor of all Indigenous peoples.

Another interpretation by Richard L. Dieterle through his interpretation of star maps in his article "The Redhorn Panel of Picture Cave: An American Star Map" is that the central figure (in white paint) is indeed Redhorn, but that his "stellar" manifestation is not simply Venus or the Morning Star but Alnilam or the fixed star of Orion's Belt.

Depending on various academic interpretations, the human head Redhorn holds is that of White Plume or his ancestor, First Father, who was beheaded after he lost his wager/battle with the Beaver Water Spirit. Together, both the Redhorn Trinity and First Father ascend from the Lower Realm back to the Upper Realm, where First Father is restored, not unlike Isis and Osiris, Mohammed, or Jesus Christ.

Dieterle's interpretation is that White Plume's stellar counterpart is the Dog Star, Sirius, and that Redhorn's stellar identity is not the Morning Star, but rather the fixed star of Alnilam, a "belt star" in the constellation of Orion.

Below is Dieterle's overlay of modern star placements on the Redhorn Panel. Besides the two figures discussed above as Redhorn, or "He-Who-Wears-Human-Head- Earrings" of Ho-Chunk, Ioway, and Otoe oral history, this pictograph is not simply an invention or exploration in art but a stellar map, carefully detailed from the heavens and translated into a broad cosmology.

To the lower right, the two figures are of deer, the larger one inverted, perhaps to represent it has been slain, as we see an arrow in its side. Dieterle's interpretation is that it is symbolic of the Pawnee stories of the creation of day and night. A smaller deer, a fawn, is also represented. While the central Redhorn figure is often associated with Venus, this star map, the very first star map found in the Western Hemisphere, details a much more complex story.

Dieterle's interpretation is that this star map pictograph can only be understood by studying the combined stories of the Indigenous peoples, the Dhegiha, Chiwere, and the Hocagara, who were there somewhere around 1000 CE. In the Ho-Chunk rite of the Society of Those Who are Blessed, there are the Heroka, perhaps "little people" who served at the least as hunting spirits, to whom Redhorn is the chief.[7]

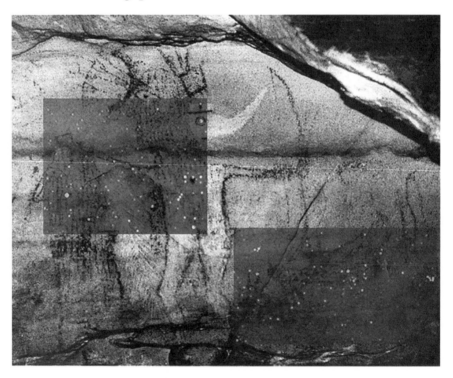

Fig. 1.6. This is a "map of the stars" superimposed over a 1,000-year-old pictograph that illustrates the Pawnee people's continuous reverence for the stars and their movements. The constellations are not astronomically correct, but they signify the one that is important for Pawnee "Star Lodge" stories.
From "The Redhorn Panel at Picture Cave with Stellar Imposition."
Hotcakeencyclopedia.com. Image courtesy of Richard L. Dieterle

Since time immemorial, human beings have used parables to tell important stories, perhaps only the very important ones. Christians have the parables of Jesus, and they cherish them. Muslims have Mohammed and the four caliphs, and the teachings of Buddha are renowned.

The Redhorn Panel of Picture Cave illustrates the power of this story of Ascension of First Father back to the Upper Realm. And because it was such a central part of the ceremonial cycle at the city center of Cahokia, it was celebrated in the outlying "cities" in the wake of Cahokia. Picture Cave is one of those outlying cities, and fortunately, we have the pictographic record to give us a glimpse of this world, no longer lost after a thousand years.

AN ISLAND IN THE EAST

*A Comparative Analysis of an
Indigenous Atlantis*

One of my fondest memories of growing up as a Cherokee youth was the sights and sounds of the Stomp Dance. My first memory was at a birthday celebration for Charlie Soap, held out by the Cherokee Nation headquarters and not at a proper stomp ground, but an introduction, to say the least. There was a fire and the words of the caller, and then the staccato but measured sounds of the turtle-shell shakers, and then watching the first seven men and women in the line come counter-clockwise around the fire, the voice of the caller leading and the men responding with their melodic refrain or response.

It was not until I was of age that I began to venture to the Stomp Grounds around Labor Day, or Redbird's birthday, but I began to understand a deeper meaning to the wonderful things I saw or heard. I enjoy all of the Stomp Grounds, but I was attracted to the discipline and structured traditionalism that was exhibited at the Cherokee ceremonial Stomp Dance grounds respectively called Redbird and Stokes, the membership rules, the adherent use of Cherokee, the careful selection of leadership.

Ultimately, I was present for a retelling of the creation story of the Cherokee, where this story was shared:

A long time ago, the ancestors of the Ani Gaduwa'gi, (People of Kituwah, a Mother Town) or Cherokee, originally lived on a large island in the East, surrounded by a great body of saltwater, and the island had volcanoes. On this island there were large and sacred turtles. Eventually, the water and the volcanoes would prove to be too much for the island, and soon the waters swallowed the island whole. The Cherokee had to flee quickly, and they were dismayed at having to abandon the one sacred Fire.

Now this fire was not just any fire. The Creator had told Thunder to put fire into a sycamore tree on an island, protected by a race of giants, the Fire People, to guard the sacred fire. All the animals, insects, birds, and reptiles called a council meeting and decided that one of them must get the fire. They would help the humans. They all tried and failed: Bear, Snake, Raven, Crow, Buzzard, and even Owl. Finally, they let Water Spider go, and she made a clay pot for the ember and could cross the water and save the one sacred Fire for the Cherokee people.[1]

In another of these Cherokee stories, recounted to me by David Scott and L. S. (Little Snow) Fields, there is one regarding several large turtles that occupy the island. In my recollection, they were very large and powerful creatures, deliberate, if not slow. The giant turtles seem to be on a mission all their own, and the teachings were not to interfere with their sacred, secret mission. But soon there were a few young male warriors who took notice and could not conceal their curiosity, and they took up the chase with the lumbering giants. Even though they were warned, they began to play on and ride the turtles' backs, hopping on and off, as the turtles began to head toward the coast and the lapping waves of the ocean. Soon, as all the boys joined in on the hoax and were all riding the sacred animals, the turtles' shells began to emit some type of sticky secretion, and try as they might, the boys could not escape from the backs of the turtles, and they were taken from this world as the turtles completed the next stage of their journey into the crashing waves of the ocean.

The moral of the story, as conveyed to me, was that the turtles are symbolic of religion, and that they are not playthings. Do not jump on and off sacred things; if you do, you will learn a hard lesson.

These stories always struck me in a spiritual way that it has taken me some years to be able to express. The story began to speak to something within me; it began to stir something old and ancient inside of me, waking up old and sacred knowledge. And with respect to the story of the Island in the East, I always would try to envisage what that great island would have looked like. I have seen the volcanoes of Guatemala and wondered what this great island in the middle of the Atlantic looked like.

Several Cherokees and I have tried over the years to imagine what it looked like and wondered how far back into antiquity we must go to know when we inhabited that island. And what happened to it? What caused the island to be swallowed up by the sea? Was it rising sea levels post–Ice Age? Was it destroyed by a massive tsunami?

And this story is not restricted to the Cherokee but is held by the other Iroquoian-speaking tribes. Many Algonquian-speaking tribes also have the story of coming from an Island in the East.

In my research, I began to find lots of comparable stories of flood narratives, including of course the Judeo-Christian flood of Noah, but also narratives that detail earlier floods and cataclysms, those that involve perhaps either geological causes (e.g., earthquakes) or cosmic causes (e.g., comet strike) of a water-based cataclysm.

Charles Hapgood (1904–1982) was a university professor as well as an author of several books: *Earth's Shifting Crust* (1958), *Maps of the Ancient Sea Kings* (1966), and *The Path of the Pole* (1970) describes his hypothesis of a fifteen-degree pole shift every twenty to thirty thousand years that takes approximately five thousand years to complete, with the most recent pole shift occurring around 9600 BCE. That would coincide with other dates for the flood and the warming after the last ice age or the end of the Younger Dryas event.[2] Dismissed by most of the academy, Hapgood's work was encouraged by Albert Einstein, who wrote the foreword of *The Earth's Shifting Crust* in 1955.

Earlier, the German meteorologist Alfred Lothar Wegener hypothesized the Pangaea world continent, pointing out that the bulge in South America fit nicely into its mirror image counterpart of Africa in a 1915 book entitled *The Origin of Continents and Oceans*.[3] Whether there was a Pangaea that eventually broke up into our continents today is hardly even refuted in the present day. So, why would the plates not have the ability to shift, perhaps so dramatically as to affect the axis of our planet and change the poles of the Earth? There are so many mysteries of our planet that we do not understand, and who is to say that there was not an Island in the East that many of our tribal Native American stories say we come from?

In my pursuit of the Island in the East I soon rediscovered the writings of Plato, specifically *Timaeus*, a dialogue supposedly having occurred around 600 BCE. I looked to one of the best interpreters of Plato's works, Lewis Spence (1874–1955), who wrote no less than five works on Atlantis, and I found solace in his multidisciplinary approach, which ranged from "mythology and comparative religion to geography, geology and archaeology."[4]

In his foreword to the work, Spence conveys the purpose of the dialogue, in which Critias tells Timaeus and Socrates that his "great-grandfather Dropidas knew the traditions of the earliest Athenians, which he had received from the wise Greek priest Solon, who in turn learnt them from an Egyptian priest of the goddess Net at Sais. This goddess was the same as the Greek Pallas Athene, and Solon claimed that she founded Athens . . . about 9600 BCE. According to the Egyptian priest, this ancient Greek city was invaded by the people of a great island in the Atlantic."

The story continues in *Critias,* Plato's second work about Atlantis, in which "War broke out between the nations within the Pillars of Hercules and those beyond them. Athens placed herself at the head of the Eastern peoples, and the Kings of the isle of Atlantis led the Western races. Atlantis was an isle greater than Asia and Lybia together."[5]

Plato detailed "the way of life of the ancient Atlanteans, their religion, cities and social customs, and how their country sank beneath the waves because of the evils of the people." The story continues, inferring that the Atlanteans became too diluted with human bloodlines and were no longer able "to carry their prosperity with moderation," and thus, Zeus summoned all the gods to a meeting in his palace. And this is where the Atlantean dialogue ends, as Plato never completed the third installment, *Hermocrates*.[6]

However, Plato describes the island nation, and it was at this juncture that I began to become intrigued, after an initial detailing of how "the god divided the earth into portions, both great and small, and to Poseidon or Neptune, god of the sea, had been awarded the isle of Atlantis, where he begat children by a mortal woman."

Cleito, his wife, "environed the mountain with mounds and ditches. The mounds were two in number, and the three ditches, which were filled with water from the sea, were placed at an equal distance one from the other and rendered access to the mount impossible."[7]

And it was from this description that I began to get curious about the connection between the two stories: both islands in the Atlantic, destroyed by a flood, with the knowledge and the people scattered, if not destroyed. After this description, however, I was drawn back to one of the renderings by Squier and Davis from their work on the ancient earthen works, and things began to click!

But while Plato's dialogue ended, the story of Atlantis is compelling, because it tells of not simply another, earlier civilization but one that affects multiple different cultures and locations across the globe.

Much was made of this depiction of the terminus of a larger serpent

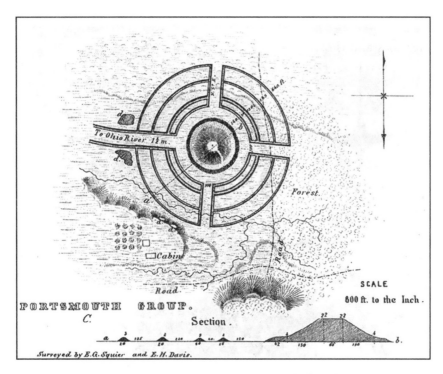

Fig. 2.1. This image shows an ancient earthen work that closely resembles
Plato's description of Atlantis in the *Critias* and *Timaeus*.
Squier and Davis, *Ancient Monuments of the Mississippi Valley*, 1848

mound, as it seemed to fit Plato's description of the home of Poseidon,
or Atlantis.

Spence's work goes on to delve into the details of Atlantis, as interpreted from Plato's dialogues.

> The god reared in the enchanted place five pairs of male children,
> twins, of whom he was the father. . . .
>
> He bestowed on his eldest born the maternal domain . . . the
> name of the eldest son was Atlas, who was king of the entire island,
> and from him the Atlantic Ocean takes its name.[8]

A most interesting approach to what might have been the Atlantis
culture comes from author Gavin Menzies, whose works *1421: The*

Year China Discovered America, 1434: The Year a Magnificent Chinese Fleet Sailed to Italy and Ignited the Renaissance, and *The Lost Empire of Atlantis* details early mariners and their visits to America and other "uncharted" areas of the world, even though many Eurocentric thinkers are still stuck on Columbus "discovering" America or rather which "civilized" sailing culture was the first to colonize the New World under the sovereignty of a religious crown.

Of course, this perspective is haunted by the looming vestige of its Indigenous inhabitants of the entire of the American continent, which by some counts are estimated in the tens of million, with a moderate range being around 50–70 million, and liberal estimates being upward of 100 million inhabitants. My theory is that smallpox, if not bubonic plaque, hit the Americas somewhere around 1300–1400 and devastated the Indigenous populations. If the North American Indigenous smallpox epidemic of the 1500s to late 1800s is any proxy, these blights and disease took between to 50–90 percent of the population, as evidenced by the smallpox epidemics of 1800, 1830, and 1860. Imagine the devastation in your own community if any significant percent of any localized population was lost. Imagine the distrust among neighbors and the wholesale loss of communal advancements.

Menzies begins with clues left in an obscure Venetian map by Zuane Pizzigano. The fifteenth-century map shows Europe, Puerto Rico, and Guadeloupe, but even maps like this one were drawing on older maps. Who drew them? Menzies fingers the Chinese, who "discovered" America before the Europeans and had sailed to Australia 350 years before Captain Cook.[9]

Much of Menzies's journey in *The Lost Empire of Atlantis* starts with his explorations of the islands of Thera and Crete and of the Minoan culture that is responsible for city sites like Phaestos, which housed the advanced civilization that included "building palaces with paved streets, baths and functioning sewers . . . intricate water-piping systems, water right drains, advanced airflow management and even earthquake-resistant walls. . . ."[10]

Menzies makes a strong argument that Minoan artifacts have been found in many parts of the world and that the Minoan culture was largely a trading society, with seafaring routes reaching many parts of the world.

Menzies also points out that the destruction of the Minoan islands of Crete and Thera was from "massive volcanic eruptions" in circa 1450 BCE. The explosion at Thera was the largest in over twenty thousand years and created a tsunami with waves reaching over eighty-five feet. He thus equated this event with Plato's description that Atlantis was destroyed "in a single day and night," and then followed by a "terrible darkness." This would be the same outcome as that caused by a volcanic explosion and ensuing tidal wave.[11]

The above would not contradict the idea of an "advanced" society that was described by Plato in *Timaeus* and *Critias,* and Plato makes the curious reference that Atlantis was covered with brass, silver, gold, and orichalcum (a copper alloy).[12]

But if the possibility of discovery of the Atlantis trade empire were not enough (which helps us validate the possibility of many Iroquoian and Algonquin migration stories that parallel the story of Atlantis), Menzies describes the content of the trade, as to unveil the economic motivations for the rise of the Minoan trading empire: bronze.

Beyond the "Treasure . . . [which] came from as many as ten different Bronze Age nations . . . gold and silver jewelry and a cornucopia of rich fruits and spices, as well as a huge amphorae from the Lebanon, terebinth resin, used to create perfumes . . . Baltic amber from the north; ebony wood, hippopotamus teeth and elephant tusks from equatorial Africa . . . Cyprus for copper, Egypt for gold," there was ingot of tin as well, which comprised nine parts copper to one part tin, and you have the raw materials for brass and the base formula for what was the beginning of the Bronze Age.

Bronze forged from nonarsenic copper and tin makes weapons with sharp edges, shields, and swords that would outlast any other weapon made before and are "strong but not brittle . . . malleable, can be cast into a myriad of shapes," even large saws to cut stone.[13]

In retrospect, we see the beginning of the Bronze Age, with its ability for its peoples to create superior weapons to win land wars and a fleet to win sea battles, but superiority in warfare is not enough to build an empire. An empire needs trade and commerce and an economic competitive advantage over others; to dominate, an empire would need a trading fleet that could cover vast distances quicker and with more cargo than its rivals. The Minoans had both trade and commerce.

The Minoan culture also had the tools to hew great stones into temples, pyramids, and burial chambers. Like the makers of the railroad tie, spike, and rail, the Minoans founded a trading empire that the rest of the world needed. They traded in all things beautiful from the corners of the world.

The Bronze Age all fueled this, but there was one small problem in the economic formula: it was not sustainable. To make the coveted bronze, you needed not only sustainable amounts of tin and copper (which the old world was rapidly diminishing), but you also needed the fuel to meld them, and that, like building massive fleets of seafaring trading ships, required trees—massive amounts of cypresses for building keels and planks and masts and lots and lots of wood to forge the bronze. Whether then or now, there are only so many trees to hew, and if there is no long-term strategy to replace them, you will, eventually, run out of supply.

Was this the end of Atlantis? Regardless, the possibility of a great antediluvian civilization being lost long ago in the Atlantic Ocean is a hypothesis that could have seeded the Neolithic cultures that were responsible for the earthen and stone works across northern Europe, as well as perhaps seeding the similar earthen works of North America.

We are all related, are we not?

THE FOUNDERS' DILEMMA
OF AMERICA

*A First Peoples' Historical Perspective
of America*

MAN WAS CREATED TO DRESS THE EARTH, AND
TO CULTIVATE HIS MIND, AND GLORIFY GOD.

*The Following is found in an ancient History of Connecticut.
Soon after the settlement of New-Haven, several persons
went over to what is now the town of Milford, where
finding the soil very good, they were desirous to effect a
settlement, but the premises were in the peaceable possession
of the Indians, and some conscientious scruples arose as to the
propriety of deposing and expelling them.*

*To test the case a Church meeting was called, and
the matter determined by the solemn vote of that sacred
body. After several speeches had been made in relation
to the subject, they proceeded to pass votes—the first was
the following: Voted, that the earth is the Lord's, and
the fullness thereof. This passed in the affirmative, and,
"Voted, that the earth is given to the saints."—This was
also determined like the former . . . 3d. "Voted, that we*

*are the saints," which passed without a dissenting voice,
the title was considered indisputable, and the Indians were
soon compelled to evacuate the place and relinquish the
possession to the rightful owners.*

EVENING AND MORNING STAR,
JUNE 1832

Native Americans and Native America are the most misunderstood people and nation in North American history.

But why are Americans today so misinformed about the real history of this continent and its original inhabitants? Why isn't the real, tragic history of Native peoples taught to every child in every state? Most Americans do not even know how Native peoples were dispossessed of their original homelands through the violation of every treaty enacted by the United States. Most Americans do not realize that many states and cities are named after tribal nations or tribal leaders.

I seek to explain not only the underpinnings of British and, subsequently, American expansionist policies that enabled the wholesale taking of a country from its Indigenous populations, but also the ensuing psychological justifications of the settlers who colonized America away from its original inhabitants, or as I have dubbed it, the "Founders' Dilemma of America."

From a European perspective, America was a New World, a place of bounty and abundance ordained by God for the puritanical Pilgrims to flourish in. As often stated in the language of the time, leaders such as John Winthrop referred to Indians as "cultural inferiors," "barbarians," "savages," "pagans," and in the extreme, "devil worshippers." These derogatory terms sought to dehumanize Indigenous populations, much like Spanish claims of Indigenous cannibalism, to better "justify their displacement and conquest."[1] A paradigm was in place, and the model would be replicated by others that followed. The origins of American paternalism are rooted in the earlier policies of European monarchies to legitimize their expansionist colonization from Europe to the Pacific Islands, South America, and ultimately, the New World of North America.

The first expansionist blows to traditional Indigenous lands came in the 1455 papal bull *Romanus Pontifex,* written by Pope Nicholas V to King Afonso V of Portugal that approved Portugal's expansion into lands they wanted to claim along the coast of West Africa. This papal edict allowed not only the seizure of non-Christians' lands, but also repeated the proclamations of an earlier papal bull, *Dum Diversas,* which allowed for the enslavement of non-Christians. While not designed for the coming exploration into the West, the papal bulls sanctioned the eventual enslavement of the Indigenous people of the New World as European monarchies vied for lands there.[2]

Following Christopher Columbus's exploits in the West Indies, the 1493 papal bull *Inter Caetera,* issued by Pope Alexander VI, ratified the right to New World expansionism (after the fact) by granting to the Catholic Majesties Ferdinand and Isabella of Castile "Discovery" rights to all lands to the "west and south" of a meridian line one hundred leagues east and south of any of the islands of the Azores.[3]

In 1792, the United States secretary of state Thomas Jefferson cited the papal bulls as the international "precedent" to justify the U.S.'s taking of Native American land.[4] The "Doctrine of Discovery" was further established in United States judiciary case law by Chief Justice John Marshall's majority opinion in *Johnson v. M'Intosh* (1823), which transferred the ownership of British lands in the Americas to the United States:

On the discovery of this immense continent, the great nations of Europe were eager to appropriate to themselves so much of it as they could respectively acquire. . . . as they were all in pursuit of nearly the same object, it was necessary, to avoid conflicting settlements, and consequent war with each other, to establish a principle which all should acknowledge as the law by which the right of acquisition, which they all asserted, should be regulated as between themselves. . . . The history of America, from its discovery to the present day, proves, we think, the universal recognition of the principles.[5]

This is the politics of dispossession; broadly speaking, America's founders had to justify their claim that they "discovered" America, liberating it from a nomadic savage and bringing civilization to a savage landscape and a savage people. Otherwise, the claims to America are illegal, immoral, and dishonorable.

But the stage was being set early on in Europe, as economic desire for colonial empires and their potential wealth grew. Accordingly, the European mindset was also set to be primed. Spaniard Juan Ginés de Sepúlveda, in a series of public debates around 1550 over the legitimacy of the Spanish war and conquest of the Americas, contended that "even the most civilized native inhabitants of the Americas were a lower form of humanity, by nature slaves."[6]

Conversely, from an Indigenous decolonization perspective, Indigenous peoples of North America, whose populations were devastated by European diseases, watched the early English visitors nearly starve, only to be saved by Indigenous "foodways, work methods, and technology," and were rewarded with indentured servitude and, ultimately, chattel slavery.

Yes, slavery. This is not what we think of when we think of the purity of the Pilgrims. The fabled origins of "American exceptionalism" have been idealized through scholarship of New England, which has "reconstructed the compelling narrative of the Puritan migration, the complexity of the English immigrants' rich religious and intellectual life."[7]

First legalized in Massachusetts Bay Colony in 1641, colonists enacted slavery laws "to define the legal status of the hundreds of Pequot Indian captives incorporated into their households." As a peculiar institution, "it flourished for nearly two centuries in the densely populated areas of English North America."[8]

Arguably, slavery became a "significant ingredient in colonial warfare rather than a footnote to it. If not the sole cause of the Pequot War, the taking of Indian captives quickly became one of its chief purposes." By the time of King Philip's War of 1675, fear and frustration among the Narragansetts, Niantics, and Mohegan over slavery helped fuel the flames of the war, not to mention the same fear and frustration was a major catalyst for the Wabanaki conflicts of 1676–1749. Following the wars, many New Englanders turned to the courts for subjugation of their so-called labor, imported them from the southern colonies, or claimed free Indians as slaves. Before 1700, Indigenous slaves were the dominant form of nonwhite labor, only to be outpaced by African slaves after 1700.[9]

The true culprit in the decimation of Indigenous lifeways were European diseases, which led to the easy overthrow of Indigenous economies and national alliances. Diseases included smallpox and, potentially, the bubonic plague, chickenpox, cholera, influenza, diphtheria, malaria, measles, scarlet fever, sexually transmitted diseases, typhoid, typhus, tuberculosis, and whooping cough. The impact of these diseases on populations with little to no immunity was devastating. On the Great Plains, between 1837 and 1870, more than four of these diseases hit in concert with each other.[10]

Lewis and Clark estimated that in eastern Nebraska in 1804, there were fewer than 7,000 Indians left (500 Otoe, 300 Missouri, 900 Omaha, and 4,800 Pawnee). This was based on earlier writings by James Mackay, who claimed that the Omaha in 1795 "boasted of 700 warriors," which roughly translates into approximately 2,000 tribal members.[11] The difference in population was due to the smallpox epidemic of 1800–1801. This was the first of three waves, the next coming in approximately 1830 and then another in the 1860s. Imagine the devastation to the cultural framework of any society but especially one based on oral knowledge transmission of seeing 80 to 90 percent of the population decimated by disease.

The larger question is how many Indigenous were here historically? How many died to disease and when? Jake Page, in his work *In the Hands of the Great Spirit: The 20,000-Year History of American Indians,* tackles some important issues but not the highly debated topic of pre-Columbian populations in the Americas.

Of the conservative estimation methodologies, A. L. Kroeber of the University of California utilized a method that sought to distinguish the ancient from the recent by interviewing living people, dubbed "informants," in a process he referred to as an "ethnographic present." He then tried to measure the impacts of disease and epidemics to arrive at a conservative answer of at least one million.

Conversely, liberal estimation methodologies, like those used by Henry Dobyns from the University of Oklahoma in the 1980s, took Spanish explorer Cortez's estimates of the population of Mexico when he arrived, and then compared those populations' aftereffects of the smallpox epidemics, which were realized a hundred years later. The result: nearly 95 percent of the population was seemingly decimated due to the ravages of smallpox.

Using this methodology, Dobyns extrapolated that Indigenous populations in what is now the United States were around 18 million in 1492 and overall, throughout the continents of North and South America, were around 112 million, with the greatest proportion of those populations located in what is now Mexico and Central America. Considering the localized population that was decimated in Nebraska by smallpox, as cited earlier, these high casualty rates are not unbelievable.[12]

To all the Indigenous youth of any of the tribes of North America, realize what a miracle you are, just by being alive. That our ancestors survived so much grief and devastation for us to be here today, is a miracle!

THE ARCHITECT OF DISPOSSESSION

President Thomas Jefferson, the father of American westward expansion and the architect of the Louisiana Purchase and the Lewis and Clark expedition, began with a seemingly benign approach to federal Indian policy, writing in 1786:

> It may be regarded as certain that not a foot of land will ever be taken from the Indians without their own consent. The sacredness of their rights is felt by all thinking persons in America, as in Europe.[13]

But this public land policy began in the years prior, before Jefferson left for France to be the United States minister. Jefferson led an effort with Congress to craft these land acquisition policies, which were enacted in the form of the Land Ordinances of 1784 and 1785 and the Northwest Ordinance of 1787.

The Land Ordinance of 1785 began with good intentions toward enacting a humane policy:

> The utmost good faith shall always be observed towards the Indians, their lands and property shall never be taken from them without their consent, and in their property, rights and liberty, they shall never be invaded or disturbed, unless in just and lawful wars authorized by Congress; but laws founded in justice and humanity shall from time to time be made, for preventing wrongs being done to them, and for preserving peace and friendship with them.

When Jefferson returned to the United States in 1789, he continued his role in the dark game of dispossession by somehow legally taking the lands, although the well-intentioned approach outlined in the 1785 ordinance was replaced by the policy of getting unqualified representatives to sign in place of the rightful leaders of the tribes. The unjust policy was evidenced in the treaty signed at Fort Harmar, which ceded nearly all the present state of Ohio. Officially, none of the tribes impacted sent representatives in protest.

But as time went on, Jefferson began to feel the pressure for more land and his desire for an agrarian farmers' economy for the nascent country, what little was left of his idealistic perspective began to waver, as he accounts in a letter to the governor of the Indiana Territory, William Henry Harrison, on February 27, 1803:

> But this letter being unofficial, and private, I may with safety give you a more extensive view of our policy respecting Indians . . . be glad to see the good and influential individuals among them run in debt, because we observe that these debts get beyond what the individuals can pay, they become willing to lop them off by a cession of lands . . . should any tribe be fool-hardy enough to take up the hatchet at any time, the seizing the whole country of that tribe and driving them across the Mississippi [sic], show only condition of peace, would be an example to others, and a furtherance of our final consolidation.[14]

This patently evil and immoral design by one of the Founding Fathers set the stage for what would soon follow, the shock waves of human behavior inspired by federal Indian Policy of the age.

What began as political motivation for an expanding, land-hungry nation, these political trends began to evolve into a "scientific" pursuit with vast social implications for Indigenous peoples.

By the time the American photographer Edward S. Curtis began his seminal project in *The North American Indian* from 1900–1930, he was heavily influenced by two prevailing ideological themes of his era: manifest destiny and social Darwinism.

Social Darwinism, or cultural "survival of the fittest" theory, not to mention the burgeoning field of Eurocentric superiority imbedded in the eugenics movement in America to conveniently characterize America's original inhabitants as less fit, went so far as to conveniently predict that Native Americans would soon be extinct and were therefore a "vanishing race."

After the end of the Civil War, the only thing left between manifest destiny and the exploration of the great West were the Indians. Samual Bowles, a New England newspaper editor, details his views on Indians.

> We know (the Indians) are not our equals; we know that our right to the soil, as a race capable of its superior improvement is above theirs; and let us act openly and directly our faith. "The earth is the Lord's; it is given by Him to the Saints for its improvement and development; and we (Anglos) are the Saints." . . . Let us say to him, you are our ward, our child, the victim of our destiny, ours to displace, ours also to protect. We want your hunting-grounds to dig gold from, to raise grain on, and you must "move on" . . . but so long as we choose, this is your home, your prison, your playground.[15]

The turn of the nineteenth to the twentieth century saw not only the federal Indian policy of allotment but also manifest destiny and U.S. expansionism on the rise. The year 1898 saw the annexation of the Hawaiian and Samoan Islands, as well as much posturing of U.S. economic might in Central and South America, especially in Nicaragua, Panama, Haiti, and Mexico.[16]

Manifest destiny, a term generally accepted as being coined by the columnist John O'Sullivan in 1845, was defined by the historian Frederick Merk as "a sense of mission to redeem the Old World by high example . . . generated by the potentialities of a new earth for building a new heaven."[17] The first time it appeared in print was by the annexation advocate Jane Cazneau.[18]

Thus, the way was paved to take over the land of the former inhabitants; the building of the American empire could not be stopped.

ANTHROPOLOGY IN AMERICA: THE HANDMAIDEN OF FEDERAL INDIAN POLICY

The origins of the field of anthropology are telling in understanding the bias afforded Native Americans. Inspired in part by the Cabinets of Curiosities,* anthropology served as justification for the often theft of artifacts from across the British colonies and areas of conquest. On a visit to the British Museum in London, visitors are exposed to the wide range of loot brought out by conquest and justified now by the field of anthropology. Their collections range from the Mayans to Roman Egypt and everything in between. What better way to justify a collection than to create a science around it? Scientific racism was just ramping up during the later quarter of the 1800s, with "human zoos" driven by anthropologists such as Madison Grant, the infamous eugenicist who put a Congolese pygmy, Ota Benga, in the Bronx Zoo and titled him "the missing link."

While Grant's scientific racism was rooted in Nordicism, a specific version of Eurocentric superiority, the institutionalization of scientific racism were embraced by the nascent field of American ethnography, or anthropology. The schools of American "cultural relativism" expanded to the field of anthropology after Franz Boas began exploring the premise that there was not a direct connection between culture and race, that the relationship was relative, and therefore what might be barbaric to some is civilization to others and vice versa. But it was Lewis Henry Morgan who would leverage the ideas of J. W. Powell (discussed later in

---

*Objects often included as belonging to natural history (sometimes faked), geology, ethnography, archaeology, religious or historical relics, works of art (including cabinet paintings), and antiquities. Cabinet practitioners in Europe formed collections that were precursors to museums.

this chapter) about the degrees of "savagery, barbaric and civilized" used to measure Native peoples and therefore propagated policies that would allow the divestment of Native rights and, ultimately, our sustenance and land.

There are two camps regarding the understanding, or misunderstanding, of Native Americans: that of American anthropology, best epitomized as the John Wesley Powell Doctrine of American Ethnology and Anthropology (not to be confused with the similarly named doctrine of former U.S. Secretary of State Colin Powell) of the Bureau of American Ethnology, versus that of Native voices, best expressed by the late Vine Deloria Jr.

The Powell Doctrine was named after its illustrious progenitor, John Wesley Powell, the first director of the Bureau of Ethnology of the Smithsonian Institution, later named the Bureau of American Ethnology, to distinguish it from its British counterpart. Powell had much to admire: he was a decorated Civil War veteran, was maimed at the Battle of Shiloh,[19] fought at Vicksburg, and was named as major during the Atlanta campaign.

Powell was also interested in the natural sciences, especially topography and geology, and after the war he accepted a post in geology at Illinois Wesleyan University and served as curator at the Museum of the Illinois State Natural History Society before deciding to explore the expansive American West.

This is what Powell is most remembered for—the series of expeditions he led into the Rocky Mountains and along the Green and Colorado Rivers. Perhaps Powell was one of America's first naturalists, lovers of wilderness and the West? The biographer Donald Worster writes in *A River Running West: The Life of John Wesley Powell.*

> Like a great river in floodtide, American in the nineteenth century
> flowed across the continent with more power and force, much of
> it destructive, than any river of nature. Powell was part of that

flow. He was enthusiastic and optimistic about where that river was heading. Although he dreamed of a different and better nation, he believed in its essential goodness. The expansion of America framed his childhood experience, inspired his adult career, and even became, as it did for so many of his fellow citizens, a personal religion.[20]

Then there is another perspective in which John Wesley Powell emerges in a different light, one in which there appears to be some deeper motivation, for while Powell "explored the Colorado River, he explored Native peoples, becoming for a period the nation's foremost authority on them. His work on Indians helped bring a shift in national policy from one of warfare and removal to one of peaceful integration and assimilation, with all the ethnocentric limitations that such a shift implied."[21]

As the prevailing notion of the day, assimilation became the most effective weapon in destroying tribal cultures, ultimately leading to punishments for speaking tribal languages and adhering to tribal life practices. Despite the ultimate outcomes of forced assimilation that Powell innately supported, he was still revered by the American public, who viewed him as an explorer and an American icon. And yet the ironies of his perspective are confounding.

Powell abhorred slavery "not merely because it was incompatible with a system of free white labor but because it was wrong to turn another human being into a commodity to be bought and sold."[22]

Yet, Powell's admirable tendencies appear to have been buoyed by something much stronger and deeper and ethnocentrically philosophical.

> . . . it was a great thing to destroy slavery, but the integrity of the Union was of no less importance: and on and beyond it all, was to be counted the result of the war as an influence which should extend far into the history of the future, not only establishing in North America a great predominating nation, with a popular and

powerful government; but also as securing the ascendancy of the Anglo-Saxon branch of the Aryan family, and the ultimate spread of Anglo-Saxon civilization over the globe. Perhaps it is only a dreamer's vision wherein I see the English language become the language of the world; of the science, the institutions, and the arts of the world; and the nations integrated as congeries of republican states.[23]

Despite his Eurocentric leanings, by 1873, Powell was hired by the Bureau of Indian Affairs to investigate the "conditions and wants" of the Great Basin Indians, despite not having any background in the nascent field of anthropology or ethnology. Powell brought the photographer John K. Hillers with him as he explored the Southwest, where Hillers succumbed to the pressures of a Eurocentric mindset, as he began to show Native peoples in stereotypical poses and even adorned in headdresses (not culturally appropriate for them as they were not Plains Natives), to promote the "noble savage" symbolism that would dominate the portrayal of Native peoples during the late 1800s and early 1900s.

Not unlike the curiosities and oddities movements in Britain, America's version of anthropology was not much better, rooted as it was in American curiosities. Powell's own office touted "a stuffed plains Bison, a Rocky Mt sheep, an extinct great auk, a gorilla's head; assorted Indian and Eskimo artifacts . . . (and) locks of presidential hair."[24] The founders of American anthropology were all new to the field, and even Powell himself was trained in geology. The whole study of Indians was a "mess . . . along with Army doctors, warriors, engineers, missionaries, explorers, and commercial travelers had all added to the pile and the confusion. . . . There was nary a PhD program in the field of anthropology until Franz Boas set one up at Columbia."[25]

Yet the nascent field of anthropology was born, and soon enough, Powell's superiors became interested in protecting the ancient earthen works built by the "Moundbuilders." It was debated who had built these works, as many felt the Native savages could not have engineered the complex mathematics. Powell himself regarded the contents as "vulgar curiosities," but did not agree that only Europeans could have built them.

The first publication of the Smithsonian was *Ancient Monuments of the Mississippi Valley* by Squier and Davis, and Powell and Powell, in his role as the head of the Bureau of Ethnology and the Smithsonian, was quick to weigh in through his paper entitled "On Limitations to The Use of Some Anthropological Data."

> In the monuments of antiquity found throughout North America, in camp and village sites, graves, mounds, ruins, and scattered works of art, the origin and development of art in savage and barbaric life may be satisfactorily studied. Incidentally, too, hints of customs may be discovered, but outside of this, the discoveries made have often been illegitimately used, especially for the purposes of connecting the tribes of North America with people or so-called races of antiquity in other portions of the world. A brief review of some conclusions that must be accepted in the present status of the science will exhibit the futility of these attempts.[26]

Here, in the first publication of the Bureau of Ethnology, Powell sets the tone for what would later be described as the Powell doctrine, the foundational cornerstone of "case law" within the academy of ethnology, later to become the field of ethnography, later to become the field of anthropology. This article would set the boundaries on what topics were off limits to the field of anthropology, such as "connecting the tribes of North America with people or so-called races of antiquity in other portions of the world." Additionally, the paper introduced into the language of ethnography the terminology of "savage and barbaric" cultures of Native Americans versus the "civilized" nature of the colonizing Europeans.

ON DISCOVERY

Similar in its ethnocentrism, the Powell Doctrine is like the Columbus Discovery doctrine, which disregards the two to three million Natives living here for many thousands, if not tens of thousands, of years.

Still, the fact remains, Native peoples have been living here for a very long time, since time immemorial, many of the tribes say. It is simply an ethnocentric bias that the only true "discovery" races are the Europeans, and that Native peoples are somehow insignificant and do not matter. So, is there any reason I, as a Native thinker, should not "rediscover" America, claim it again as our sacred homeland, and bare its secrets to be revealed again?

Another facet of the Powell Doctrine was the Bering Strait theory, or the Clovis Horizon hypothesis, which proposed the only way for ancient Asiatic peoples to have arrived in America would have been for them to have crossed the Beringia land mass, which connected Russia and Alaska during the end of the Ice Age from somewhere around thirteen thousand years ago.

This theory is so entrenched in anthropology that those who have tried to disprove it are often met with derision and criticism. An example would be the Vanderbilt University anthropologist Tim Dillehay, whose work in Monte Verde, Chile, in 1979 challenged many accepted theories on discovery. Dillehay conducted radiocarbon dating of charcoal and bones at the site that yielded a date of 14,000 BP, which is one thousand years before the Clovis Horizon hypothesis was possible. This work was not properly accepted until 1997. Dillehay's most recent work, "Monte Verde: Seaweed, Food, Medicine, and the Peopling of South America," reinforces earlier reports with radiocarbon dating between 14,220 BP and 13,980 BP.[27] More recently, radiocarbon dating in White Sands, New Mexico, has verified Indigenous footprints from nearly 23,000 BP.

The Discovery Doctrine is an important milestone in American history, as it makes the illegal taking of this continent from its original inhabitants somehow moral by wiping out the previous history as being insubstantial enough to overlook. But through the "Indigenous lens," we can see plainly the injustice done to all who walked these lands before the European conquerors.

BY VIRTUE OF BLOOD AND BONE

Now let us move on in our journey of the Americas, and let us look from the West to the North, and there we find Vine Deloria Jr.

Vine Deloria, Oglala Lakota from Pine Ridge, was many things, but I prefer to think of him as a thought leader and contemplative commentator on behalf of Natives everywhere. A hero, even. Deloria's early work in *Custer Died for Your Sins: An Indian Manifesto* attacked the status quo U.S. federal policy of termination and called for tribal sovereignty, attacked popular nonnatives, and attacked the continued acculturation and complacency of Native peoples themselves.

Deloria's work continued attacking the ethnocentric mindset, as established by those like J. W. Powell, through works such as *We Talk, You Listen, New Tribes, New Turfs,* where he pits the individual mindset of the Western mind versus the communal nature of the tribes and concludes that tribal spirituality and neotribalism can be the salvation of the soulless nature of American consumerism. He concludes on America, "The glittering generalities and mythologies of American society no longer satisfy the need and desire to belong."

In *God Is Red,* Deloria challenges us all to answer the questions "Who am I?" and "Why am I here?"

> Almost everywhere we turn whether we be red, white, black, brown, or yellow, we are confronted with the necessity of renewing our vision of the totality of our existence, our understanding of the nature of the universe, and the paths by which we can move forward . . .[28]

However, he also explores the role of the white man. Deloria chose to turn the tables on those philosophies on "savage and barbaric" versus "civilized," coined by Powell, through the words of the Lakota chief Luther Standing Bear:

> The white man does not understand America. He is too far removed from its formative processes. The roots of the tree of his life have not yet grasped the rock and the soil. The white man is still troubled by primitive fears; he still has in his consciousness the perils of this frontier continent, some of its fastnesses not yet having yielded to his questing footsteps and inquiring eyes. He shudders still with the memory of the loss of his forefathers upon its scorching deserts and forbidding mountaintops. The man from Europe is still a foreigner and an alien. And he still hates the man who questioned his path across the continent.
>
> But in the Indian the spirit of the land is still vested; it will be until other men are able to divine and meet its rhythm. Men must be born and reborn to belong. Their bones must be fortified of the dust of their forefathers' bones.[29]

Standing Bear of the Lakota touches upon one of the great secrets of Native peoples—that we are as human beings forever tied to the land, and that pedigree is perhaps only steeped after many, many generations have fed the land with the blood of life and the bones of the departed, back into the ground, to carry the spirits back into the land.

Luther Standing Bear also calls out the disunity of the white man from the land, and the result is fear of the land, and his guilty conscience feeds his own lack of confidence over the horrible lies and treachery employed for him to steal the land from the First Peoples of this continent.

We are reminded to remember Chief Standing Bear of the Ponca, who in 1877, was forced, along with his tribe, to relocate in a diaspora to Indian Territory, only to have to return when his only son, Bear Shield, died after arriving in the "warm country." By January 1879, thirty Ponca men, women, and children went with Standing Bear to honor his son's wishes to return his bones to the land of his forefathers.[30]

So, what is the true nature of this relationship between First Peoples and the land? We know in our explorations that there is something to the antiquity of blood, bones, and the clay of the land. Both can be a deep red. As I have begun my own spiritual journey to find these answers, I have gone to the history of the written word and the living word of the elders.

From the Northeast, I have studied stories of the Iroquois, the Seneca and their ceremonies of the Little Water Society, and the Ancient Guards of the Mystic Potence, and they allude to a Covenant between the Animals and Humans. And that Covenant is based upon respect between the Animals and the Humans. And if we respect them and honor the Covenant, then they will help us, the Humans.

Within these mysteries of traditional societies, such as those from the Odawa Nation, we find a story of the Seven Grandmothers (like a Native Seven Commandments from the Creator), the "rules" of those grandmothers, and the Law of Orders; in short, it sets up a hierarchy for sustainability and balance of the Plant Order, the Animal Order, and the Human Beings, respectively.

If we Human Beings put ourselves above the other two primary orders, we will but destroy ourselves, and the other two will live on without us. We Human Beings are in a sacred balance with Mother Earth. And such a careful balance it is. Are we at present out of balance as an interrelated body of Human Beings? What teachings and wisdom can we all learn by studying the past, present, and future of Native peoples?

ON WESTERN CHRISTIAN THOUGHT

In *God Is Red,* Vine Deloria juxtaposes linear Western Christian thought with the cyclical notion of time, the notion that history repeats itself or that Indigenous thought recognizes that time passes in epochs, from one age to another.

Deloria details the history of Western Christianity, specifically that of the Catholic church, from its papal edict of 1537.

American Christianity has blood on its hands from the conquest of Indigenous lands and our teachings of being stewards of the land versus the King James Bible's ultimatum to "let them have dominion over the fish of the sea, and over the fowl of the air, and over the cattle, and over all of the earth, and over every creeping thing that creepeth on the earth," and that blood is of Mother Earth.

> The contemporary Christian mythos has been developed over a period of two centuries in which the exploitation of human and natural resources became increasingly sophisticated . . . in its propensity to missionize, Christianity has avoided any rigorous consideration of ecological factors in favor of continuous efforts to realize the Kingdom of God on earth.[31]

Herein lies the primary difference between Red and White thought. Do we as Human Beings have an inherent right to dominion over all the Earth? Or are we, more honorably, stewards for the short period each of us must live on Mother Earth? Deloria offers us the beginning of a new philosophy and a different approach to dominion, which has left Human Beings bereft of respect for the Mother, greedily devouring her resources in a shortsighted vision that does not pass the "Seven Generations" filter of the Iroquois, which states, "Any important decision must bear the impact upon the next seven generations," as paraphrased to me by my late mentor, Principal Chief Wilma Mankiller. More on that later.

The most poignant piece of *God Is Red* resides in Deloria's call to the land and, most importantly, to sacred land. He achieves this by contrasting the "temporal and spatial terms" with the "linear" notion of time in Western thought. Deloria points out that all things that are sacred to Native peoples begin and continue forever through what I refer to as sacred geography, whether it be a "river, mountain, plateau, valley or natural feature," and the existence of holy places confirms tribal peoples' rootedness, which Western man is without."[32]

Deloria binds sacred geography to us in our everyday life of Native peoples through ceremony. "Are ceremonies restricted to particular places, and do they become useless in a foreign land?" This reminds me of a conversation with Osage spiritual and prayer leader Roadman Andrew Gray of the Native American Church. "The old folks told me to not take my Fireplace across the river, we never went across the Arkansas River."

Deloria leaves us with a challenge that we need to revive our "dreamer societies," "healing ceremonies," and "divination and foretelling . . . discovering the future."[33] Christianity and its associated boarding schools stamped out these mystical societies. Deloria challenges Native peoples to revive these societies to get us back in tune with our older cosmologies and teachings as Native peoples.

> One of the greatest hindrances to the reestablishment of tribal religions is the failure of Indian people to understand their own history. The period of cultural oppression in its most severe form (1887–1934) served to create a collective amnesia in contemporary people. . . . Tribal people are in the unenviable position of dealing with problems the origin of which remain obscured to them.[34]

But Deloria also has a challenge for non-Native peoples as well. In his conclusion to *God Is Red,* Deloria challenges non-Native peoples to practice a form of neotribalism, but he does not elaborate. My interpretation of this notion of neotribalism is not for non-Native peoples to imitate Indigenous but to think more tribally, to have a deeper connection to the land, to learn to respect the plants and the animals as brothers and sisters, to acknowledge that they, too, have souls and spirits, and to worship the glory of Mother Earth.

In the epitome of the Western tradition, we have the beginning as Creation (in seven days, no less) and the end with the destruction of the Earth. Is this enough spiritual magnetism for all? Are we destined for our heaven to be a mythical place? Can we not find in our own hearts, the "heaven on earth" right here, in this wonderful gift of the Creator, our own Mother Earth? Why not celebrate the beauty and mysteries of the Mother, rather than depleting the forests? Are the forests not like her lungs and the oil, gas, and shale her bowels? How much can she, the Mother, take?

Until we can find a guiding theology in America, and this globe for that matter, that respects our planet and all its ecosystems, our long-term existence as a species is limited.

Do we as Native peoples have spiritual guidance for others? This is a complex and sometimes controversial question for Native peoples. On the one hand, most true traditionalists would never sully our spiritual lifeways by proffering them for profit. This includes shamans and anyone masquerading as a commercial spiritualist. Even as I write this, I realize the careful balance I must maintain with respect to the sanctity of our spiritual lifeways and the natural desire to share healthy aspects of our teachings with others.

And then there is prophecy.

The Prophecy of the Seventh Generation leads us into one of two ways as human beings: either we unite as a species in the long-term preservation of Mother Earth, or we perish.

I believe that an Earth-centric life philosophy is well overdue. When all the creatures (including us) find a common vision to embrace the diversity of the planet and recognize pantheism, that God is in everything, that all is sacred, including the Plants, Animals, and Sacred Spaces—the tribal unit is key to maintaining this balance—then we might have a chance.

LIVING RED

An Indigenous Philosophy on Living in Harmony
with Earth Mother

THINKING RED

Living Red began as a thought, a spark, a rekindling of something deep inside of me—something long lost but not completely forgotten—or at least to somewhere in the blood that runs through my veins. Most certainly it was a feeling, a reawakening to the ancient past, combined with my own personal physical connecting with Mother Earth. Thinking Red starts with the supposition that Mother Earth is more than just the land, the water, or even the wind.

Thinking Red begins with an understanding that one is quite small in the bigger picture of life, that we are indeed dependent upon the earth for life. When I was growing up in tribal communities, a common phrase was "water is life-giving." I would often hear the women in my tribe, when making water blessings, start their offerings acknowledging that all of God's children, all the two-legged, all the four-legged, the winged ones, all of us, needed water to live. Those water women would pray for those who lacked water to drink and those who lacked clean water, and they would cry in empathy for those souls, and they would thank the Creator for water that they had drunk in their lives and thank the Creator for every drop of water that they might have in the future, and they humbled themselves in reverence.

Now, I understood those words they were saying and what they meant, I mean the literal translation. I think most can understand the words, but did I truly understand what they meant? At first, I thought they were somewhat stating the obvious, acknowledging that we all need water. Of course, we do, and we need the air to breathe, but no one ever acknowledges that. We all take that for granted, do we not?

At first, it rubbed me the wrong way, and I am not sure why. Perhaps because I felt it was oversimplifying something that happened every day for every single creature. Was I subconsciously angry because I knew there was something powerful in those prayers that I didn't understand or that I didn't want to acknowledge? Most of mainstream society takes water and air for granted, and I had never thought much about it not being there. All I had to do was breathe and oxygen was there or turn on the tap and let water pour into my glass, or shower in it, or wash my vehicle, or water the lawn . . . And somewhere in that logic, or illogic, I began to see the hypocrisy of what most Americans take for granted. That we can continually take from the Earth, like a greedy and precocious child, and expect it to never run out. I, too, was guilty of taking water, air, the environment, and even the gas in my vehicle for granted.

What if there came a time when water, clean, pure water, was gone? Wasn't there a time when we could drink water from not only springs, or deep wells but also from our creeks, rivers, and lakes? Today, most cringe at the thought of drinking water from rivers and lakes, but were the rivers and lakes not polluted by the runoff from our industrial and agricultural waste? Why can we not seek to have pure waters again? If we can destroy the sanctity of water, then we can rebuild it. In our infinite ability to create, I know we can make most waters potable again.

I refer to the teachings I learned one cold winter in Saskatoon, Saskatchewan, with Cecil King, PhD, of the Odawa Nation, a part of the Algonquin confederacy. Cecil shared many things with me, but one really resonated.

I look to the teachings of the Odawa for an explanation of the Law of Order. The Plant Order is the first priority in the sacred balance of the world, then the Animal Order is second, for the animals depend upon the Plant Order for survival. And as the most unique of all the Orders, the Human Beings, we must subordinate ourselves to both the Plant and the Animal Orders, or we will simply destroy ourselves. This is the prophecy of the Law of Orders.[1]

The teaching of the Indigenous peoples of the Americas, regardless of the tribe, or in which nation-state they reside, or what language they speak, is to remember that we are indeed meant to be stewards of this planet, not to rule over her in dominion.

RED LANDSCAPES AND RESTORING ECOSYSTEMS

Thinking Red is about developing an understanding of the environment around you. And, perhaps, not even what it is today, but rather how it used to be. I tackle this issue in other portions of this work, but the face and landscape of America have been radically altered since the European conquest of America from its Indigenous roots. And by that we can talk first about how this landscape was changed by the massive loss of millions of true American bison, from oak savannas with buffalo grass and bluestem fields pervading the landscape to replacement by the ever-present multitudes of genetically modified fields of corn and soybeans.

This transformation has its roots in the Jeffersonian notion of yeoman farmers in an agrarian utopia driving our economy and giving the young America an identity. This transformation also gave a nascent United States a "reason for being"—to take over the "unproductive" lands left foolishly "idle" by the Indigenous tribes, thus adding value to a "wild wilderness." And while this transformation of the literal landscape of America gave purpose to many early Americans to physically transform them into "productive" lands, the unfortunate reality was that this transformation was at the expense of the natural flora and fauna of this continent. Is that "progress"? Or, in our thought process at the time and our desire to assert dominion over all things, have we destroyed much of the beauty that was naturally created by the Mother, for us and our sustenance?

Is it time to start thinking about a world where we might try to restore our ecosystems to a previous glory, to do our part as human beings to restore a sacred balance that was once here, which must include the Native American tribal heritages that lived alongside this landscape for hundreds if not thousands of years? Can we restore the grains and vegetables that sustained us, can we not restore the oak savannas and the prairie ecosystems so that the Bison, the Elk, the Wolf, and the great Bear might roam the lands the Creator made for them and us? Can we empower the Native American consciousness to look back into the past and into our souls, to find again in our hearts those sacred teachings that were once bestowed up on our Native ancestors, and then share them with the world, if even by example, for that is what is necessary to save the planet? These are our teachings, our prophecies.

There are some absolutes that need to be challenged if we are to come to an understanding of what Living Red is. The first tenet is that we must understand that Mother Earth is alive, a living organism, and that there is a special relationship between humans and this sacred, special planet.

THE EARTH AS OUR MOTHER: THE BONDS OF BLOOD AND BONES

In other portions of this work, I refer to our connections as Human Beings with the land, that there is a relationship between the land and the blood and bones of our ancestors. Why would there not be? If the

Mother is indeed alive, a living, sustaining organism, then why would there not be a relationship between the Earth and the Human Beings that live among her creations, as the Earth sustains us with what we need to live: water to drink, air to breath, and the Plant and Animal Orders to sustain us?

I started this work challenging the Old Testament's Genesis 1:26, "And God said, 'Let us make man in our image, after our likeness: and let them have dominion over the fish of the sea, and over the fowl of the air, and over the cattle, and over all of the earth, and over every creeping thing that creepeth upon the earth.'" I challenge this part of the Bible, not as a statement against the veracity of the work, but more as a sudden realization that if we could only truly understand the powerful and complex beauty that is the living organism of Earth, if we could discover that we, as Human Beings, can in fact complement and enhance nature and make its bounty and bosom even more pronounced rather than seek to drain it of its resources in the vain hope of short-term wealth, then we can do our part to save Mother Earth!

Is it so daring to acknowledge a special relationship between the Earth and the bones and blood of one's ancestors? Would the Mother not know her progeny? Would not our souls, which are immortal while our human vessels are not, recognize the land that sustained them and all of the other immortals' souls? To quote Chief Seattle, in his retort to the signing of the Treaty of Medicine Creek in 1854:

> To us, the ashes of our ancestors are sacred, and their resting place is hallowed ground. . . . Our dead never forget the beautiful world that gave them being. . . . Every part of this soil is sacred in the estimation of my people. Every hillside, every valley, every plain and grove, has been hallowed by some sad or happy event in days long vanished. The very dust upon which you now stand responds more lovingly to their footsteps than to yours, because it is rich with the blood of our

ancestors and our bare feet are conscious of the sympathetic touch. Even the little children who lived here and rejoiced here for a brief season will love these somber solitudes, and at eventide they greet shadowy returning spirits.

And when the last Red Man shall have perished, and the memory of my tribe shall have become a myth among the White Men, these shores will swarm with the invisible dead of my tribe, and when your children's children think themselves alone in the field, the store, the shop, upon the highway, or in the silence of the pathless woods, they will not be alone. At night when the streets of your cities and villages are silent and you think them deserted, they will throng with the returning hosts that once filled them and still love this beautiful land. The White Man will never be alone.

Let him be just and deal kindly with my people, for the dead are not powerless. Dead, did I say? There is no death, only a change of worlds.[2]

These hallowed words, spoken so many generations and years ago, hint at secrets that might be lost on many of you, perhaps on many of the Indigenous peoples of today. But the hint is that there is indeed a physical connection between the blood and bones of tribal peoples in the Americas (or, at the very least, their DNA) and the physical earth in which they are interred. For those of us who believe that we have immortal souls, they are indeed tied to the land that our Indigenous teachings tell us is sacred.

I found that passage from *God Is Red*, by Vine Deloria Jr., and he was a stalwart for so many of us. A giant, even. Deloria's work has influenced me so (for more on this topic, see chapter 3), and I wanted to expound some more on his influence over me.

It took me several attempts to understand *Custer Died for Your Sins*. At first, I thought it was a lauding of the Red Power movement of the late 1960s and the early 1970s, and I still refer to it as a manifesto. But as I grew older, I was able to compare it to the subsequent *God Is Red*. I first read *Custer Died for Your Sins* in my college years, and it went over my head. I tried again in my thirties and realized it was much more than a political manifesto to the Red Power movement, that there was more to it, but I couldn't put a finger on it. Finally, in my forties and alongside *God Is Red*, I began to understand more.

What I was able to finally understand about both of Deloria's early seminal works was that Deloria was taking his understanding of the Christian liturgy afforded to him via his own father, Vine Deloria Sr., an Episcopal archdeacon and a missionary on the Standing Rock Reservation, and his grandfather, Tipi Sapa or Black Lodge, who was also a member of the Episcopal clergy. In *God Is Red*, Deloria lays out the different philosophical perspectives of the Western American Christian versus the Native American conceptions of time and space. The Western perspective is linear in nature and historically was able to control the narrative.

In contrast to this linear, revisionist perspective of the conqueror, Deloria describes the cyclical nature of time in Native concepts and worldviews. There are indeed cycles, and this reminded me of the prophecies, the Seventh Fire of the Algonquin, the Seventh-Generation prophecy of the Dakota, and their messages and prophetic stories of hope, regeneration, and cooperation to save ourselves from ourselves and somehow save this planet, our Mother. I was at first hesitant about the fatalistic nature of this worldview, because it struck me how many would have to suffer, the generations of suffering.

I think of the suffering that befell my own ancestors, what a mathematical rarity I am, that my ancestors survived genocide and near extinction because of disease, and destruction of everything that provided them sustenance, including nearly all the animals and many of the indigenous plants. It struck me how lucky I am to be here at the point of deep despair and yet somehow be alive to see firsthand some of the prophecies of the Seventh Fire and the Seventh Generation unfold in front of my eyes.

My journey in Living Red began with a seed. But your journey may begin differently. Every story and every journey will be different. If the journey is to connect with something bigger than yourself, to help us do everything we can to protect Mother Earth and the sanctity of her sacred spaces, then we are on the same journey.

LIVING RED: PROTECT THE SACRED WATER AND PLANT THE SEEDS OF RESISTANCE

In April 2014, the Cowboy and Indian Alliance's week-long "Reject and Protect" #NoKXL campaign included a powerful march on Washington, DC, and had a tipi encampment on the National Mall that ultimately got the attention of the White House. But the nod from the White House was not what impressed me. This "Reject and Protect" campaign rallied some of the best leaders I knew, such as Casey Camp-Horinek of the Ponca Nation. Casey is a traditional Ponca tribal leader whose knowledge of culture and history is as grounded as her capacity to inspire a crowd with her words and song. I knew Casey from her family's traditional dances and pristine ceremonies that the Camp family sponsors year after year.

When I was told the Poncas were coming up to plant sacred Red Corn in the pathway of what would be the Keystone Pipeline, I was more than intrigued. Red Corn is sacred to both of our tribes and is, for the most part, a true vibrant red variety of heirloom corn indigenous to Nebraska that had been lost to the Omaha. More on this later, but the right and responsibility for the keeping of the sacred Red Corn in the Omaha tribe is left up to the *Inke'sabe* or Black Shoulder clan, the Earthen Moiety Buffalo Clan, to which I belong. I was on board.

I will forever remember that day, my first time up at Art Tanderup's farm outside of Neligh, Nebraska, eight miles up County Road 857, to be exact. It was there that I met a host of people I would come to know and respect. I met Ben Gottschall that day. Ben is a real cowboy who runs an organic grass-fed cattle outfit with his father, Jerry Gottschall, who also runs an organic bison operation. I had asked Ben, "Where are all of the Poncas?" and he said he didn't know, but that Jane Kleeb, one of the leaders of the "Cowboy and Indian Alliance," had planned the Indigenous interactions. Ben and I were shooting the breeze when I saw a plume of dust coming up the long driveway, a white truck stained with the "red dirt" of Otoe/Ponca country down in Oklahoma.

Once stopped, the truck's back doors opened and a horde of little Ponca grandkids came pouring out of the truck, followed by two large imposing figures in T-shirts. The plates on the truck were from the Ponca Nation. A small but important fact here is to understand that the Ponca and the Omaha tribes are very close kin. Regardless, our language is almost identical, so on impulse and hope I said hello and asked them how they were, in our language. And much to my surprise, and to theirs, they responded back in our language. Complete strangers but speaking our ancient language, we bonded immediately.

The first Ponca relative I spoke with was Amos Hinton, and I discovered that his role within the tribe was to take care of the Ponca Nation's agricultural endeavors, but his companion said he was a Keeper of the Corn for the tribe. *Mi'ka'ci* "Coyote" Camp was his companion, and he looked like a brawler with his muscular build. Amos would tell me later that Mi'ka'ci was the Pipe Carrier for the Ponca Sun Dance ceremony. I was blessed to meet them.

I would learn during our interactions that day and our friendship in fighting the Keystone XL pipeline that the sacred red corn they carried had come from Amos researching what happened to the corn that lay fallow in the fields that fateful year of 1877, when the Ponca Trail of Tears occurred. Amos was able to track that some of the sacred red corn had been picked up by the neighboring Yankton Sioux and put in a medicine bundle. Amos was then able to track the bundle through descendants of the Yankton bundle keepers, and then a trade occurred to have the corn returned to the Ponca. The corn that we planted in the path of the Keystone Pipeline was the corn from over 137 years ago. Art had been concerned that the Ponca were gambling all their sacred corn on his farm; he was concerned that it wouldn't grow after all those years. But Amos reassured him that it would grow, and over two-thirds of the corn did grow that year.

Part of me thinks it has to do with the ceremony that occurred that day. Just Amos, Mi'ka'ci, and I took care of it and they had me do the main prayer. Humbled, I spoke what I could of our sacred language in prayer to the Creator. Somewhere along the way, the Thunder Beings heard our pleading and granted us thunder and rain as a blessing. All the non-Natives were running for their cars, and Amos made me run after them to tell them it was a blessing, and it would pass. It did, and we planted that sacred red corn that day, and I know in my heart our ancestors smiled down on us.

Fig. 4.1. Seeds of resistance: two Keepers of Corn and a Pipe Carrier. Amos Hinton (Ponca Keeper of the Sacred Corn), Taylor Keen (Omaha Keeper of the Sacred Red Corn), and Mi'ka'ci Horinek (Ponca Sundance Pipe Carrier). Taken at the residence of Art and Helen Tandrup, October 27, 2015.
Photo courtesy of Taylor Keen

THUNDERBIRD EGGS AND
THE WATER WALKER WOMAN

In most of our Indigenous worldviews, water belongs to women. I believe this is because women hold the water of life, the ability to give life. The sacred feminine ties water to the moon in many tribal cultures.

The late Anishanabe Grandmother Josephine Mandamin (often called The Water Walking Woman) was inspired to start water walks, leading many women to traverse the banks of many waters, specifically the Mississippi River, praying for the sanctity of these waters.

So, in the winter of 2017, I was a witness when Grandmother Josephine recounted a story. She spoke of an Ojibwa woman from the Serpent River tribal community, who had a dream about the Thunderbird Egg that had found its way to her. It was conveyed that the desire was to have someone place the special Thunderbird Egg stones in the waters of the Missouri River near the Dakota Access Protest. It seemed an honorable task, so I told Grandmother Josephine that I would go with her.

I believe in all our tribal stories, especially the ones involving these cosmological deities. The Thunderbirds, in our ancient Indigenous narratives, are described as rulers of the Upper Realm, yet are also the messengers of the Thunder Beings. Some of our stories say that they live in the great western cedars near the Pacific Ocean, and some of our stories say that when lightning strikes a certain type of tree, then at the roots the eggs are born. Most of the tribes have these Thunderbird stories, regardless of the story. In the Omaha tradition, they occasionally show up protecting someone or something.

The stories are not unlike the dragon stories of Europe, such as the "fire-drakes" of Beowulf, who not only breathed fire but were also seen to glow at night. These dragons "often had horns or antlers and/or a sort of mane . . . like a horse's head . . . some . . . covered with feathers and often with wings . . . serpent like."[3] The Asian dragons were often associated with "rain and often depicted as wise and benevolent," not to forget the stories of the Mayan Kukulcan and the Aztec Quetzalcoatl.[4] Often in the European version, such as in the battle between St. George and the dragon or the young Merlin's white and red dragons, they appear to be symbolic of something more, perhaps Anglos versus Saxons or Christianity versus Paganism.

There are parallels between them, something linked as well to the stories of the Phoenix in the lost gospels of the Bible. From the Third

Fig. 4.2. Rulers of the Upper Realm and dutiful messengers to the Thunder Beings; Thunderbirds' wings clap thunder and lightning emits from their eyes and talons.

Artistic interpretation courtesy of Isiah Stewart (Lakota/Mohawk)

Book of Baruch, which is not unlike the tale of the Book of Enoch, a heavenly host descends to our realm to reveal to Baruch "all the mysteries of God . . . during which Baruch discovers the mysteries of creation. He learns . . . about the operations of the sun and moon, the origins of the rains, and the great serpent which drinks from the cosmic sea to prevent it overflowing."[5]

I had mixed feelings about visiting Standing Rock. It appeared to be loosely based anarchy. I kept looking for elders, and saw many seemingly lost souls looking for, what, I do not know. The reaction from the state police was militarized and overkill.

Regardless, we had a mission to complete, and I was blessed to help Grandmother Josephine complete her task. I wondered later that night what it might be like to see a Thunderbird flying over the protest site, wings flapping like thunder and lightning emitting from its eyes. Maybe in another dimension or realm, it was really happening.

PAHUK

Sacred Geography in Nebraska

Late Spring, 2016.
Somewhere outside of Fremont, Nebraska

At first, the weather never seemed to want me to visit Pahuk—too cold, then too rainy. Summer was nearly upon us when my guide, Cherrie Beam Clark, the longtime caretaker of the Pawnee sacred geography effigy mound complex, Pahuk, and I finally made my introductory and exploratory journey. The mosquitos were out in full fury, and flowers flowed out of the landscape wherever one looked. We were clearly out in the middle of nowhere—rural Nebraska.

Everything along the way to Pahuk was flat and slowly turning bright, verdant green. The path was slick with freshly wet clay. We struggled across the former pathways now grown over, letting the Plant Order slowly take over again.

Before we ascended the final hill, Cherrie stopped to challenge me, perhaps unknowingly, perhaps not.

"You know all of the other Indigenous that I have brought up here knew instinctively the exact place to pray."

"So, this is a test?" I questioned, a bit caught off guard.

All I got was silence in response, as we continued our trek and moved up the slowly rising and undulating landscape. At the top of the climb was a flattened plateau, a vast circle where the wind blew broadly. In awe, I watched a herd of deer bounding across the landscape. My eyes

Fig. 5.1. The entrance to the Pahuk plateau is framed by a large and powerful oak tree, the Pawnee Tree of Life.
Photo courtesy of Taylor Keen

finally settled on a large, iconic, and powerful oak by the entrance to this large plateau, the tree itself enshrined by beautiful flowers.

"The Pawnee Tree of Life," Cherrie proclaimed.

I approached the tree carefully, but with exuberant anticipation, put down tobacco, and said a prayer. I touched its bark, hoping it would share a gem of knowledge with me.

When I touched the Tree of Life, pressing myself close to its bark, it felt electric. It started something within me, a chain reaction of sorts.

I liken it to a series of memories connecting and of planting the corn, singing to it, watching it sway in the light of the setting sun, then following the cycles of the sun and moon to plant the Three Sisters of corn, bean, and squash.

Those deliberate acts have changed me. Profoundly. Not just bringing light to my heart and spirit, but also bringing a sense of peace and grounding me as I am finding my way back to things once forgotten. They are revived again, with sanctity and sacredness.

Stepping away from the Tree of Life, Cherrie and I turned and walked across the broad plateau. The wind whipped around us, creating a cacophony of sounds from the birds, the wind, and the rustling grass. Once we reached the far side, I felt a tingle in my stomach as I saw the plateau break off. A shelf of earth lay below us, overlooking the serpentine bend of the river.

"This is it," I announced.

"Very good," said Cherrie. "I will leave you alone. Come find me along the path when you are ready."

I rooted myself on the earthen shelf, feeling the wind blow over and through me. I felt the presence of many ancestors. Closing my eyes, I could begin to see a world forgotten. A time long past and yet very much alive.

Prior to visiting Pahuk, I had heard rumors of this land. When I met the current landowners, they spoke of its power but seemed to be reticent about details, or perhaps they felt this place was not theirs to interpret.

My friend and guide, Cherrie, had befriended the earlier owners, Lou and Geri Gilbert, "at the height of the hippie days" in 1975. Cherrie had been intrigued after hearing of a couple that "lived off the land and could forage in the woods for food." Cherrie said, "I had to figure out a way to meet them. I finally called one day and asked if I could come out and see their place, because I enjoyed organic gardening. They invited me out, and we were instant friends."[1]

Cherrie recounted how it was Geri who fell in love with the place simply because, as Geri told Lou: "I just want to walk in the woods. I just want to be here." Lou, also known to many as Dr. Gilbert, ran a successful urology practice in town.[2] At first the land was a refuge from city life in Lincoln, but then, in Cherrie's words, "buying the place completely changed their lives. As golf-playing, country club people from Lincoln, they suddenly changed and started learning about insects and native plants and birds."

Over the years, Cherrie told how the Gilberts, "restored thirty-eight acres of tallgrass prairie, made five miles of hiking trails, and cleaned

Fig. 5.2. Upper Plateau, Pahuk.
Photo courtesy of Taylor Keen

old garbage and junk cars out of the ravines. The most beautiful part about the Gilberts is they refused to allow anyone to call them owners of the land. They called themselves caretakers. They took their roles as guardians of this special land very seriously and passed that on to me. It became an arboretum site and the Gilberts received numerous awards for habitat restoration and protection."[3]

Previously, the Gilberts had only vaguely known of the land's sanctity to the Indigenous, as their real estate agent had mentioned that in the past the land had "something to do with Indians." However, after Dr. Gilbert went to the Nebraska State Historical Society, the Pahuk connection was made, and the site was put on the National Register of Historic Places. Pahuk was the very first conservation easement with the Nebraska State Historical Society.

Cherrie carried on the Gilberts' work as the caretaker of Pahuk for the greater part of thirty-five years. This piece of geography was particularly important to the Pawnee people, formerly of Nebraska and Kansas, now relocated in Oklahoma, and she took it upon herself to bring back a group of Pawnee elders. She spent almost seven years knocking on the doors of Pawnee elders, down in Oklahoma, before she gained their trust. By 1994, she had successfully worked with the Nebraska State Historical Society to achieve her goal.

Very little has been written about Pahuk, and very few people know about it outside of the Pawnee Nation. What has been documented by anthropologists is not always easily discernable for the common reader. Many non-Indigenous writers miss the mark when it comes to understanding sacred geography, whether it be directly by misappropriating Indigenous cultural iconography or indirectly by tainting the work with a Eurocentric bias. I was pleasantly surprised by the deftness of non-Indigenous author Peter Nabokov.

Nabokov's book *Where the Lightning Strikes: The Lives of American Indian Sacred Places* addresses Pahuk and documents some of the further history of this wonderful place. In his research, Nabokov relates the story of the Berkeley linguist, Doug Parks, who in 1965 wandered onto the Pawnee reservation in Oklahoma to study Caddoan, the language family of the Pawnee.

Here, Parks found a willing and dedicated man by the name of Harry Mad Bear. He was "a blind man . . . a stalwart Baptist and member of the Native American Church . . ." To Parks, he was "an exacting informant, after each session . . . Mad Bear would press his ear to the tape recorder to check the jaw-breaking words and intricate syntax." By the end of 1970, Parks had taped thirty-six stories. Parks continued his work with another tribal elder, Nora Pratt, and they added more narratives from a Pawnee named Roaming Scout and began to analyze them.[4]

While Mad Bear and Nora Pratt were not born in the Pawnee homelands of Nebraska, they could recount quite a few stories. Parks put together the pieces and realized the story most referred to was about Pahuk.

Another early academic in the field of ethnology was Melvin Gilmore. Gilmore did interesting and helpful work in the field of ethnobotany as well as in the nascent field of ethnography. In another Pawnee elder account told to Gilmore by *Letekots Taka,* or White Eagle, it was said that in the days of sacrifice, a man sacrificed his beloved son to Tirawa, the Creator, by slaying him with a knife and throwing his body into the Platte River, where it eventually drifted downstream to Pahuk and was spotted by two buzzards, who saw his body and, "carrying the boy on their backs, . . . placed him on the ground on top of the bluff over the big cave, which is the home of the Nahu'rac. In this lodge were all kinds of animals, and all kinds of birds."[5] Bears, mountain lions, bison, elk, beaver, otter, deer, and all kinds of birds were represented in the Nahu'rac.

> There is a little bird, smaller than a pigeon, its back is blue, and its breast white, and its head is spotted. It flies swiftly over the water, and when it sees a fish, it dives down into the water to catch it. This

bird is a servant or a messenger for the Nahu'rac. The Kingfisher pleads with the other animal spirits to restore the boy to life. It could not be decided by the Council of Animals, the Nahu'rac, and thus they ask the Kingfisher to decide, and he asks them to bring the boy back to life. "Let us teach him all we know and make him one of us." . . . They were glad. Then they began to sing, and they danced. They taught the boy all their secrets . . . to do this and to train him in the powers of the animals. Eventually the boy was made a doctor, and again was taught all that the Nahu'rac knew. After that he could do many wonderful things.[6]

Gilmore's stories about Pahuk are mesmerizing, if not haunting. However, it was Mad Bear who told of a young man named Pacha who "had the good fortune to enter the lodge at Pahuk (sic)."

Pahuk or "Mound Sitting on (or over) the Water" is a sacred place to the Pawnee and other tribes such as the Omaha, who call it *Pahe Waxube,* and the Lakota, who call it *Paha Wakan* or Holy Hill. Pahuk is considered holy ground and is the one of five underground Animal Lodges, geographically close to Cedar Bluffs, Nebraska.[7] To be considered sacred, these animal lodges all have common elements:

They occur on a riverbank, close to where a trail crosses the river.
They have a Mound that replicates the earth lodge of the animals.
They have a spectacular view in all directions from the top of the cut bank.
They all have a cave or a spring that is tied to the emergence narratives about coming from the underworld or out of water to this realm. They are located in oak tree savannas.[8]

In their article "Pawnee Geography: Historical and Sacred," anthropologists Doug Parks and Waldo Wedel describe the relationship between the animals and the celestial gods of the stars, who were the sources of knowledge and power. These animal lodges were places where "animals of all species met and conferred supernatural powers" on deserving Pawnees who had been called to Pahuk in a dream. In

Fig. 5.3. Lower Pahuk by the Platte River,
near the Effigy Mounds portion of the complex.
Photo courtesy of Taylor Keen

more than one case, the path to these animal lodges is initiated by a creature of the Lower Realm, a "water monster," who either in dream or by its "powerful breath, drew the man into the river and into the animals' lodge. There the man was taught the secrets of the animals."[9]

To understand these sacred sites, one needs to understand the relationships of all. With respect to the Skidi Pawnee, we begin with the celestial bodies, "the stars, the sun and the moon were subservient to *Tirawahat*," the Creator of the universe, who assigned each of these celestial bodies to their stations, much like the Upper Realm. These Upper Realm deities were instrumental to the creation of our world and to maintaining a balance. "Certain stars created the first human beings, each of whom was believed to be a founder of a Skidi village, its first chief and keeper of its sacred bundle."

The animals of our realm were the intermediaries of the power and knowledge of the Upper Realm, to confer on us humans, if they saw fit. The patron star of the Animals was the Black Star in the East, who watched over the Animals and gave them the power to confer medicine on humans, who "became mysterious and were like the animals" with curative powers and "able to cure disease or illness . . . to perform feats of magic."[10]

But how did the people find themselves underground? The Arikara, relatives of the Skidi Pawnee, have an emergence story that is related. "The world was originally occupied by giants, but Nesaru, the Creator, wiped them out with a flood, saving the smaller people by placing them in a cave underground with Mother Corn, the mother of the tribe."[11]

In her book *Love Song to the Plains,* Mari Sandoz said, "Here, as old Pawnees used to tell the story at evening fires":

Once, long ago, all things were waiting in a deep place far underground. There were the great herds of buffaloes and all the people, and the antelope too, and wolves, deer and rabbits—everything, even the little bird that sings the tear-tear song. Everything waited as in sleep.

Then the one called Buffalo Woman awoke, stretched her arms, rose, and began to walk. . . . Everywhere as she passed there was an awakening, and a slow moving, as when the eyes were making ready for some fine new thing to be seen. Buffalo Woman walked on in the good way, past even the farthest buffaloes, the young cows with their sleeping yellow calves. She went on to a dark round place that seemed like a hole, and she stood there a while, looking. Then she bowed her head a little, as one does to pass under the lodge flap, and she stepped out. Suddenly the people could see there was a great shining light all about her, a shining and brightness that seemed blinding as she was gone.

And now a young cow rose and followed the woman, and then another buffalo and another, until a great string of them was following, each one for a moment in the shining light of the hole before he was gone, and the light fell upon the one behind. When the last of the buffaloes was up and moving, the people began to rise too, one after another, and fell into a row, each one close upon the heels of the moccasins ahead. All the people, young and old and weak and strong went so, out through the hole that was on Pahuk, out upon the shining, warm and grassy place that was the earth, with a wide river, flowing below, and over everything a blueness, with the tear-tear bird flying toward the sun, the warming sun. . . . The people looked all around and knew this was their place, the place upon which they would live forever, they and the buffalo together.[12]

I had hoped to experience this sacred cave, but it has been taken back by the river and time.

With these stories, I look much differently at the landscape of Pahuk. From that first moment when I approached the Pawnee Tree of Life until I looked over the vast panoramic plateau, I felt the wind blow in my face and watched several groups of deer bounding like distant jackrabbits in the far distance.

But all is not lost. There still stands an old burr oak, thought by the Pawnee elders to have been there when the "Pawnee had last visited with Pahuk" before the removal from Nebraska to Oklahoma. This is the Pawnee Tree of Life. I was blessed to see it in the full of spring, after the Thunder Beings brought spring back with their first voices of thunder.

Another Pawnee elder interviewed about the land said, "as long as the land was undisturbed, then the animal spirits and the animal lodge would all still be there, waiting for the Pawnee to return," to share again their medicine, along with all the spirits of their ancestors whose bone and blood lie in this earth, called Nebraska. Another elder explained that most of the sites had been damaged, developed, or simply torn down. Pahuk was different in that it was undisturbed. Or was it?

In January 1858, the early "founders" of Kansas Territory had intentions to build a capital for the Nebraska Territory called Neopolis over the sacred spot of Pahuk. I do not know if it was simply coincidence or purposeful ill intention that they chose the most sacred spot of the Pawnee.

It was cruel to systematically divest the Indigenous populations away from the sacred homelands where they had lived for thousands of years, but it would have been far worse a crime to build a capital on the place most sacred to them. Where is the humanity for mutual respect and justice? Indigenous peoples were put here in this spot to protect Mother Earth and to respect the Covenant between the animal lodge councils, the Naha'ruc, and us, the human beings.

I believe it is high time for healing. It is time for the good people of the plains of Nebraska and Kansas to welcome back, with open arms and hearts, the descendants of the original inhabitants of these lands. I hope this action will bring healing not only for Natives of these lands, but also between all human beings, the sacred animals, and Mother Earth herself. We owe that much to the beauty and memory of the stories of these lands.

The bones and blood of the Indigenous peoples who once lived as stewards of these lands need to be reconnected with their sacred geographies. If they are allowed to take care of these sacred spots, perhaps then the plants, the animals, and Mother Earth might choose to share some of the stories of the ancient path and share her healing heavenly magic once again with human beings.

MOTHER CORN, MOTHER EARTH

Rediscovering a Sacred Tribal
Feminine Tradition

In my journey exploring the ancient earthen works, it became apparent from studies that there used to be a sacred balance inherent in the physical works, as well as a sacred balance in the old cosmologies of ancient America. I have discovered that a sacred balance also existed between the masculine and feminine powers. This balance was well represented in the earthen works, as indicated by the basic earthen work shown in figure 6.1 on page 74.

Here we have the two basic forms of sacred earthen architecture: the "point within a circle" or circumpunct, which is often associated with sun-centered cultures, if not sun worship itself, and the eight-sided square, which is oriented to the cyclical movements of the moon. In Native cosmologies, the sun is masculine and the moon personifies the sacred feminine. As we see in these conjoined henges, the eight-sided square corresponds to the phases of the moon, which is the physical manifestation of the sacred feminine as the moon is tied to the fertility cycles of women, and many of the stories of the Plains tribes correlate the intimate relationship of the moon with women and the sacred feminine.

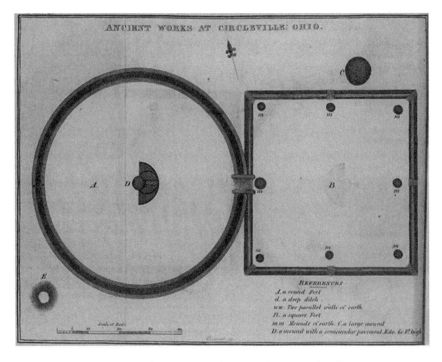

Fig. 6.1. The circular and square earthen works at Circleville representing
the conjoined sacred feminine and masculine, aligned to track the
movements of the moon and sun over time.
From *Writings of Caleb Atwater*, 1833

THE SACRED FEMININE IN THE ANCIENT EARTHEN WORKS; A STUDY IN ARCHAEOASTRONOMY

Within one of my tribes, the Omaha, many of the feminine clan names of the tribe relate to the phases of the moon, such as Mi'toN'i (new moon) and Mitexi (sacred moon). Our tribal teachings say "that the moon belongs to women" and that when the moon is full "men are not to even look at it." Our Omaha stories say the moon is filled with sacred water and "fills up and spills out every month" as it spins from crescent to full and wanes back to the opposite crescent. Omaha tribal teachings say the sacred water of the moon and its night power are tied to the "live-giving waters" of all women; "Ni'ta'wa'iN" or "water is life giving."

Upon closer inspection and study, we find that the conjoined circle

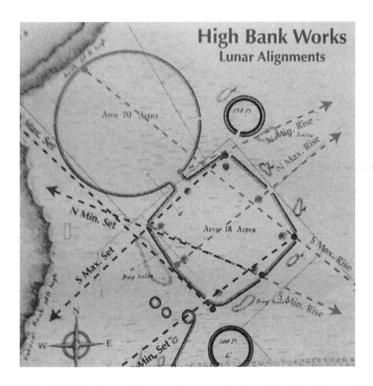

Fig. 6.2. The High Banks earthen work complex is not unlike the conjoined works of Circleville, but here the archeoastronomy is detailed with the minimum and maximum moon rise alignments in the octagon.

From *Ohio Archaeology: An Illustrated Chronicle of Ohio's Ancient American Indian Cultures.* Orange Frazer Press, Wilmington, OH, 2005. Courtesy of Voyageur Media Group, Inc.

and octagon shown here at the High Bank Works demonstrate the eight rise-and-set points of the moon that define the 18.6 lunar year cycle.[1]

Which leads us to the question: What is the sacred feminine?

Anthropologist Tim Pauketat explores the role of the sacred feminine in a set of works relating to Cahokia and migrant farmer laborer communities, where red stone carvings pay homage to the Mother Earth Goddess and to Corn Mother, recognized widely among Native cosmologies. In these "outskirt" communities, corn was a staple commodity, and some of the migrant communities were often marginalized from the elite communities in the heart of Cahokia. It was the excesses of the masculine that eventually toppled megacenter communities like Cahokia.

I believe not only that the subjugation of the sacred feminine was responsible for the collapse of these great ancient American empires, but that the loss of the sacred feminine is at the heart of unrest, war, and lack of harmony in our societies today, not simply Native American tribal societies, but all societies. Imagine a world where women held equal authority to men!

REDISCOVERING THE SACRED FEMININE

Recently, the Buffalo Bill Center of the West (BBCotW) contracted me as a cultural consultant to provide my interpretive perspective on a massive collection, the Paul Dyck Plains Indian Buffalo Culture Collection, because of my work on ancient America. While exploring the collections for common symbolism that I have studied in relation to the ancient earthen works and associated art and stories, curator Rebecca West offered to show me items that the museum had in their collection relating to the Omaha.

Rebecca carries on a strong curatorial legacy established by her and the previous curator Emma Hansen (Pawnee), as evidenced in the work *Memory and Vision: Arts, Culture, and Lives of Plains Indian Peoples.*

After I had conducted my consultancy work with Rebecca, she casually mentioned, "I would be remiss as a curator if I didn't do my homework on your tribe," as she laid a folder in front of me. The folder contained correspondence with the Omaha Nation going back over twenty years.

The first letter was addressed to my uncle and namesake, Dr. Rudi Mitchell. Very few museums really have the moral rectitude I was witnessing with Rebecca and the BBCotW relative to working with tribes. I could see the legacy that had been built over the years in relation to the Plains collection as Rebecca explained the powerful tribal advisory board they retained and the support the collective museum offers to tribal ceremonial objects and their respective tribes.

Then, Rebecca went to work on the computer, explaining her own journey at the museum, an interdisciplinary career spanning twenty years. "These items haven't been viewed in a very long time," she began.

"How do you know that?" I asked.

"Because it's primarily in the Dewey decimal system," Rebecca explained, and we both laughed! "Nineteen-sixties, nineteen-seventies, who knows," she added. "Something is confusing here . . . Some of these items seem to be tied together. But something is odd here. Please bear with me."

I waited, probably not so patiently, and soon she had thumbnail pictures. The first one that struck me was called "Wildcat Hides and Stick."

"What kind of wood is the stick made from?" I asked immediately.

Fingers typed. "Plum," Rebecca stated.

"Plum." I thought. "That's a fruit tree." I began to wonder about the sacred feminine that I had studied in my journey into the Mounds, especially having read Pauketat's latest anthology regarding Corn Mother in sacred carvings of pipestone and other red stones.

"Is there paint on it?"

More typing fingers. "Hold on a minute."

I was already on to my next question. "Is it . . ."

"It says red ochre," Rebecca answered my question as if reading my mind. "Oh my. That is sacred, for certain."

"What if we find something? Something sacred?" I inquired out loud but probably more to myself to convince myself this was really happening.

Rebecca was typing away furiously. "These objects are tied to two Calumet wands we have in our permanent collection upstairs. And there is a gourd rattle. Could you affirm if it is a peyote rattle?"

"Yes, of course I could," I added, having grown up in the Native American Church and being a fan and gourd ceremonial artist.

We found the gourd, and its design was unique, a circle around the tip third of the gourd, with four vertical lines descending on it. The paint was a dark blue.

"No, it's not a peyote gourd. May I sing with it?"

She nodded, and I sang a simple prayer song to WakoNda. I felt the electricity of time and ancient things in my hands. It tingled.

And then it all hit me—I knew where I had seen the Wildcat hides and stick. One of the anthropological books I researched was on the Pawnee Hako, or Calumet ceremony. That's where I saw them. And the Calumet Pipe Wands. And there was more, but I couldn't remember right then.

"Everything is going to be in a box," Rebecca explained. "Look in that drawer next to you."

And so I did as instructed, feeling a bit numb. I opened the drawer and saw an inscription on a box.

As I looked closer, Rebecca read from a footnote. "It says here, 'corn bundle.'"

I froze.

Bundles and packs were the most sacred of sacred objects. I recalled immediately the family story of my grandmother encountering a sacred bundle on display, encased at a local museum. I remember that she cried and spoke to it, humbling herself. And the room then filled with the sacred incense of cedar smoke. Everyone there acknowledged it to be so.

On the box was written "Medicine Pipe Dance Bundle," and I read it aloud to Rebecca. I found the Wildcat hides, covered in plastic.

"Take them out of there," she offered. And then added as her fingers quit typing, "And whatever else is in that box. Look."

And then I found her. Mother Corn.

Rebecca left me alone with her for a few minutes, as she followed procedure and went to inform the staff of the potential find. I cried tears of joy and thanked Mother Corn for having the spirits lead me to her. Thanked her for having me find her. Thinking of my journey of the recent past and planting the Three Sisters and trying to understand the sacred masculine and feminine. *What could the return of Mother Corn mean to my tribe? Could she help us heal and flourish again?*

"TO SING FOR SOMEONE" (WA'WAN)

As a part of my research into the ancient past of my ancestors, I have found that in many ways, all the tribes are related, or "ay'wi'thi'woN'gthe." Sometimes Omahas have kinships—for example, the Dhegiha Siouan-speaking cognate tribes, such as the Quawpaw, Kansa, Osage, and Ponca. But I have discovered connections on many levels, such as shared sacred geography, common teachings, stories, and in some cases, ceremony.

To the Omaha people, the Wa'WaN or Calumet was a cultural ceremony that was centered on the balance between the sacred masculine powers and the sacred feminine powers.

The Wa'WaN ceremony, or "to sing for someone" is more commonly referred to as the Calumet ceremony, which, according to the oral tradition as written down by Fletcher/La Flesche, came to the Omaha from the tribe's time at Xe—or, to some, Blood Run—in northwest Iowa and the South Dakota border by the Big Sioux River. According to sacred legend, it came about:

"While a council was being held between the Omaha, including the Ponca, the Cheyenne, the Arikara, and other tribes (Iowa and Otoe), to bring about friendly relations . . . and this ceremonial tie which should be regarded as of a nature as inviolable as that between a father and son."[2]

The anthropologist Alice Fletcher documented the Pawnee version of the Calumet, which was collectively known as the Hako ceremony, in the late 1800s. While the Omaha, Ponca, and Dakota all practiced this ceremony, by the late 1800s the Chaui band of the Pawnee retained most of it.

The origins of the sacred Peace ceremony are ancient. While often referred to as the Calumet ceremony, it is different from the East Coast Calumet ceremony. It is thought that there are two versions of this Plains phenomenon, one version with the sacred Medicine Pipe Bundle and the southern version known by the Pawnee as Hako.[3]

Based on the works of Fletcher and La Flesche in the book *The Omaha Tribe*, they allude to the legend of the sacred pole and the formation of an intertribal council of the Omaha, Ponca, Cheyenne, Arikara, Iowa, and Otoe. This council may have had other purposes regarding the sacred pole and the formation of the Hu'thu'ga (our sacred formation of our tribe in two clanships), but it is said that it was there that they devised and planned for a broad Peace ceremony that evolved into the Wa'WaN of the Omaha, "the same ceremony as the Pawnee Hako."[4]

The widespread nature of this ceremony was evident through multiple observations in the seventeenth century. Early French traders cite the Caddo practicing it in Texas, Louisiana, and Arkansas. The Omaha oral tradition tells that it was known to the Arikara on the Missouri River and was probably introduced by them to the Omaha, Ponca, Iowa, Oto, and Cheyenne at the village on the Big Sioux River.

The Arikara and Pawnee are the long-standing residents of what today we call Nebraska. Moving southward from Xe, or Blood Run, the Omaha/Ponca ultimately descended the Missouri River, and

> they found the Arikara there, cultivating the maize and living in villages composed of earth lodges—evidently a peaceful, sedentary folk. Omaha war parties from the east side of the river harassed the Arikara, who were living on the west side. The Arikara sought to obtain peace through the influence of the Wa'WaN, but Omaha war parties seem finally to have driven them from their homes and to have forced them northward up the Missouri River.[5]

The most readily identifiable objects associated with the Calumet, or Medicine Pipe Dance, are the Calumet Wands, which are sacred pipes, although there is no bowl, and they were never smoked. Yet, they are sacred, and they were spoken of as pipes and were held in the greatest reverence.

Below is a description of the Calumet Wands/Pipes attributed to the Omaha that are a part of a collection held at the Buffalo Bill Center of the West:

Each stem was of ash; a hole burned through the entire length permitted the passage of the breath. The length was seven stretches between the end of the thumb and the tip of the forefinger. The stem was feathered, like an arrow, from the wing of the golden eagle. Around the mouthpiece was a band of iridescent feathers from the neck of the duck; midway up the length was a ruff of owl feathers; over the bowl end were stretched the head, neck, and breast of the mallard duck, tied in place by two bands of buckskin painted red, with long flowing ends. Beyond the owl ruff were three streamers of horsehair dyed red, one at the top of the stem, one at the owl feathers, and one midway between.

On the stem, a "straight groove, painted the color red, that ran the length of both stems stood for the straight path, representing the path of life and was interpreted to mean that if a man followed the straight path of life the sum of life and happiness would always shine on him."[6]

These hair streamers were bound on by a cord made of the white hair from the breast of a rabbit. From each stem dangled a fan-like arrangement of feathers from the tail of the golden eagle, held together and bound to the stem by two buckskin thongs; the end, which hung from the fan-shaped appendage, was topped with a downy eagle feather.

One of these fan-shaped feather arrangements was composed of ten feathers from the tail of a mature golden eagle. These were dark and mottled in appearance and were fastened to the blue stem; this pipe . . . represented the feminine element.

The other stem, which was painted green, had its appendage of seven feathers from the tail of the young golden eagle. The lower part of these feathers is white; the tips only are dark. These were the feathers worn by men as a mark of war honors and this pipe . . . symbolized the masculine forces.

It is to be noted that among the Omaha, as among the Pawnee, the feathers which were used by the warriors were put on the stem painted green to represent the earth, the feminine element, while those which were from the mature eagle and which stood for the feminine element, were fastened to the stem painted the color of the sky, which represented the masculine element; so that on each pipe the masculine and feminine elements were symbolically united.

Near the mouthpiece was tied a woodpecker head, the upper mandible turned back over the red crest and painted blue. The pipes were grasped by the duck's neck, the mouthpiece pointing upward. When they were laid down, the stems rested in the crotch of a small stick painted red, which was thrust at the head of a wild-cat skin spread on the ground. This skin . . . served as a mat for the pipes when they were not in use and as a covering when they were being transported. The wild-cat skin was required to have intact the feet and claws, and the skin of the head.

Two gourd rattles . . . a bladder tobacco pouch . . . to which was tied a braid of sweet grass, a whistle from the wing bone of the eagle, and three downy eagle feathers completed the articles required for use in the ceremony.[7]

This excerpt is taken in its entirety from the ethnological work of Fletcher and La Flesche. As evidenced by the previous photo, and witnessed by the author, the items within the collection of the BBCotW are consistent with Fletcher and La Flesche's anthropological descriptions of the Wa'WaN ceremonial objects of the Omaha.

Interestingly, there is some controversy regarding the role of Mother Corn in varying accounts of the Omaha Wa'WaN ceremony. In their formal ethnographic report of 1911, *The Omaha Tribe,* Fletcher and La Flesche write:

> While nearly all the articles used and their symbolism are identical, yet the absence of the ear of corn from the Omaha ceremony forms the most striking difference between the two. With the Pawnee the corn is spoken of as "Mother," and typifies Mother Earth, to whom the whereabouts and fortunes of man are known. In the Omaha Ceremony the corn has no place.[8]

Yet, in 1884, anthropologist Dorsey describes Mother Corn among the Omaha, as does Fletcher herself in her own publication on the Omaha Wa'waN in 1884, referring to the ear of corn as "wa-ha-ba."

> Ear of corn, white, without blemish and very full, and called the mother. A green band is painted around the middle from which four stripes extend to the top of the ear. The ear of corn thus decorated, like the gourd and the bladder pouch, is tied around the middle by a buckskin thong to a stick about a foot and a half long and painted red.[9]

Fletcher also misinterpreted, as did Dorsey, this oversight of green versus blue. For blue represents the sky, and Mother Corn was to be anointed with the power of the Creator from the "dome of the sky."

So why would Fletcher publicly contradict herself? Depending on the provenance of the items relating to the Omaha Wa'WaN at the BBCotW, the answers might lie therein. Perhaps the sale of the Wa'WaN items away from the Omaha (1875?) might have given license to Fletcher to omit its importance in the Fletcher/La Flesche ethnographic work of 1911. Perhaps Fletcher was complicit in the dispossession of these sacred items from the Omaha people. Perhaps it was simply an innocent omission.

Another theory on the provenance of the Calumet items might lie in the striking similarities to items from the Pawnee Hako Ceremony. There is a question regarding whether the Omaha Wa'WaN ceremony is related to the Hako version of the Pawnee or to the northern version of Calumet referred to as the Medicine Pipe Dance, as the box that held the collection at the Buffalo Bill Center of the West was entitled "Medicine Pipe Dance Bundle."

Or conversely, perhaps the Hako and this Medicine Pipe Dance ceremony were one and the same ceremony. This would follow suit as the Arikara and some of the bands of the Pawnee are tribally related, in that sacred legend the Calumet was introduced to the Omaha/Ponca by the Arikara at Xe, or Blood Run.[10] The Cheyenne, Ioway, and Otoe were present as well. Regardless, the Wa'WaN ceremony of the Omaha and the Skari/Hako ceremony of the Pawnee are the same ceremony.[11]

Because of the similarities of the ceremony, the similarities of the ceremonial objects, and the yet unexplored provenance of the collection, the origin of this set of supposedly Omaha Wa'WaN could in fact be a gift of the Pawnee or the Arikara to the Omaha. Consultation with both tribes would be prudent in understanding the similarities and differences.

However, there are some unique differences that might bring some clarity to the Calumet Wand/Pipes themselves.

It is the custom among the Omaha, when preparing the feathered stems, to draw a black line near the bowl end. The line does not show, for it is covered by the neck of the duck, but it is there, with its symbolism. It represents the neck or throat of the curlew. This bird in the early morning stretches its neck and wings as it sits on its roost and utters a long note. The sound is considered an indication that the day will be cloudless. So, to all the other emblems on the stem this prophetic call of the curlew is represented as adding its song to the forces that make for the symbol of peace. In the Inke'sabe gens, which had the keeping of the tribal pipes, the name

Ki'koNtoNga, "curlew," is found. The name refers to this symbolic mark on the Wa'waN pipes.

In contrast to the black line painted on the stems of the Omaha Wa'waN pipe stems, in the Pawnee Hako/Skari version of the Calumet ceremony (to be discussed in depth later), the stems are painted the same color, but have no black line, but like the Omaha stems there is a groove carved into each of the pipe stems and painted red. The makers of these pipes are either of Omaha or Pawnee/Arikara origin, as both tribes would be candidates for a Calumet type of relationship with the Omaha.

It was my study of Alice Fletcher's work on the Pawnee Hako/Skari (Calumet) ceremony that allowed me to even recognize Mother Corn and the other Calumet ceremonial items when I saw them in the collection at the Center of the West.

First, we have Kawas, the brown feathered stem (feminine). The stem is painted blue with a paint, mixed in a "white shell" because "Tira'wa gave us the shells and gave them long life and the power to keep away disease and sickness." The white shell is used because of its simple purity and because it "once was a living thing" and it "lived in the water" and thus is endowed with the sacred feminine and is worthy of becoming the feminine pipe for peace and fertility.

The stems are made of ash, just like the Omaha Wa'waN stem. And the feminine stem is painted in blue, for "blue is the color of the sky, the dwelling place of Tira'wahut that great circle of powers that watch over man." And the masculine is painted in green, which "represents Tohaur (Vegetation), the covering of H'Uraru, Mother Earth." Both stems have a long groove carved in the stems, and after being painted blue or green, the groove is painted red "because the passageway is red through which man's breath comes and goes to give him life. The sun too is red, and the groove represents the straight path whereon the sun shines. The teachings of this ceremony make a straight path along which if a man walks, he will receive help from the powers."[12]

On both Hako pipestems, the composition of birds is the same as the Omaha pipestems: "the eagle is chief of the day; the owl is chief of the night; the woodpecker is chief of the trees."

From the composition of the "four chiefs" to their respective placement, it is like the Omaha, if not more symbolic. From the color of the paints to the straight red path, the mandible of the duck, the woodpecker head near the mouthpiece, and the owl feathers before the breast of a duck, all aspects of the Pawnee Hako/Skari Pipe Wands are akin to the Omaha ones, further clarifying a strong relationship between the two ceremonies.

As to what appears being deeply more symbolic for the Pawnee ceremony versus that of the Omaha ceremony, this could be simply a matter of experience by the author, or it could infer that the Pawnee had originated the ceremony. Alice Fletcher had written the ethnographic work *The Omaha Tribe,* with Francis La Flesche published in 1911, and having this experience with a good translator and a member of the tribe she was studying, made a good model for her writing.

To this model, Fletcher employed the help of James Murie (Pawnee), with whom she found someone who could practice the "sacred language" she had been afforded by working with Francis La Flesche of the Omaha. Through Murie, Fletcher had the opportunity to meet Tahirussawichi, a Chaui band chief who held the sacred role of the Ku'rahus, the leader and expert of the Pawnee ceremony known as "Ruktaraiwarius," which roughly translates as "they who have the breathing mouth of wood are coming." It was Tahirussawichi who had accompanied the Hako Ceremony when it "was carried by his people to the Omaha."[13]

Ultimately, the most symbolic aspect of the Pawnee Hako/Skari and the Omaha Wa'waN is the object known as Mother Corn to the Omaha and as Atira or "mother" to the Pawnee. Here, Mother Corn represented "the fruitfullness of the earth. The tip end was painted blue to represent the dome of the sky, the place of the powers, and four blue equidistant lines, running halfway down the ear, were the four paths along which the powers descended to minister to man."[14]

Mother Corn of the Pawnee was adorned with the blue markings, braid of buffalo hair and on sticks of Plum, painted with red clay, just like the Omaha. Although one distinction of the Mother Corn that was found in the "Medicine Pipe Dance Bundle" at the BBCotW did not have most of the top rows of corn still attached, and therefore no eagle plume. Whether or not this is significant, that is not known. Additionally, one can see the similarity of the gourds used in the Pawnee Hako to that of the Omaha.

ON THE IMPORTANCE OF MOTHER CORN, THE SACRED FEMININE, AND PEACE OVER WAR

Some of you reading this might ask, what's the big deal over a piece of corn? Isn't it just a symbol? How can corn be sacred?

The Calumet was an important ceremony across North America. It is one of the few truly pan-tribal ceremonies that spanned the Plains, the Southeast, and the Algonquins, and there are some ties to the Iroquoian Eagle Dance as well. One of the reasons it was so powerful was that it was a Peace ceremony, that could, in many cases, stop a war between feuding individuals who were unrelated, or more importantly, stop or prevent a war with a neighboring tribe.

THE POETRY OF CALUMET AND MOTHER CORN AND MOTHER EARTH

Back to the name of the Omaha Calumet itself. "To sing with" is poetic enough as the translation of the Omaha word "Wa'waN." From the Pawnee comes the phrase Ruktaraiwarius, "they who have the breathing mouth of wood are coming," which denotes that the wooden Pipe Wands, if not the entire "Medicine Pipe Dance Bundle," are alive. To the Osage, the ceremony was referred to as "Bringing the Drum," and to anyone who has ever been to the District EnloNska "Playground of the Oldest Son" dances of the Osage and have witnessed the passing of the Drum and the lavish gifts, one can see the potential tie to the elaborate giving ceremonies of the Calumet.[15]

Beginning with Calumet Pipe Wands, we note that in the Wa'waN and the Hako ceremonies, the hierarchy was led by the feminine wands, who always went first, having the mature feathers of a female golden eagle, while the masculine Wand was secondary in this ceremony, as it was painted green for vegetation of the Earth and it was adorned with the immature feathers of a male golden eagle, as was the role of feminine peace over masculine war in this ceremony.[16]

In addition, there was a balance to the Pipe Wands that balanced the masculine with the feminine of each pipe. The feminine Pipe Wand was adorned with the mature feathers of a female golden eagle, and the ash stem of the pipe was painted dark "blue for the sky, which represented the masculine element." Conversely, the masculine pipe, adorned with the immature feathers of a male golden eagle, was painted green

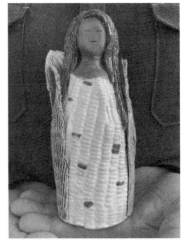

Fig. 6.3a, b. The author's artistic effort of Mother Corn, as historically interpreted by the Cherokee tradition.
Photos courtesy of Taylor Keen

to represent the feminine aspects.[17] All in all, there was a sacred balance between the masculine and feminine.

From the Hako ceremony, she was called "Atira" or Mother and represented the "fruitfulness of the Earth." The blue clay painting on the corn represented the "dome of the sky where the powers dwell."

If only we had a ceremony today that could still stop war. "Few persons ever spoke to me of them without a brightening of the eyes. 'They make us happy,' was a common saying," wrote Alice Fletcher.

Someday Mother Corn will return to the Omaha, the People Who Move Against the Headwaters, and it will be a long-awaited reunion. I hope to witness it.[18]

CAHOKIA

The Rise and Fall of an Indigenous Empire

CAHOKIA CITY CENTER, SPRING OF 1054

A young Indigenous man, a Pilgrim, has been walking all day carrying a large bundle basket on his back. His long black hair is tied up in a bun at the back of his head, and he has new, round, purplish, flint clay spools in his ears. The young man's body is taught, lean, and muscular, and a simple red loincloth is draped around his waist and through his legs, with the tail of the cloth flowing behind him.

This Pilgrim is journeying into the ceremonial city center of Cahokia from his new farming home community a couple of days walking distance away. The Pilgrim's whole family, clan, and tribe had heard the great stories of the Cahokian Empire and had left their former homelands, much farther away, to see if the stories about Cahokia were indeed true. They had found a place in one of the suburban farming collectives that paid tribute crops to Cahokia.

The stories about Cahokia are everywhere. Stories about more people gathering here than anyone could ever imagine, in a large "city," where work was done for the greater good of the city itself. Not just people living closely, but living in a new manner, for something greater than themselves.

As the Pilgrim moves closer to the city center, he passes many

Indigenous women working the fields of corn, beans, and squash. All around him is a vast floodplain, stretching for miles and miles. High along the bluffs framing the floodplain, the Pilgrim sees low burial mounds, thatch-roofed buildings with burial scaffolds, perhaps open so the dead can see the heavens. The floodplain is filled with marshy lowlands, and he passes by thousands of cattails, watercress, and duckweeds.

As the Pilgrim moves closer to the city center, the marshlands and crop fields give way to open plazas and well-trodden paths, and he sees the larger, angular, flat-topped ceremonial mounds rising out of the landscape, and smoke trails emanating from larger thatched artifices.

The Pilgrim hungrily smells the pungent feasts of deer, elk, bear, and bison meat everywhere, mixed with the sweet scent of sage, sweetgrass, cedar, and juniper incense. The sound of drums and singing looms in the distance. The Pilgrim had never seen so many people in one place, thousands upon thousands of people, all speaking different languages, and all living in peace with one another.

Everywhere there are young people like himself working on the Mounds. The platform mounds are finished with a black packed clay, but he sees various colors and textures of earthen clays and soils utilized in building up the new mounds, with many intricate layers. People are digging and seem to be leveling the glorious Grand Plaza. In other earthen works, people are breaking figurines and pottery in a ritualized manner. It seems it is all for a reason, the work itself. Everyone around him is delighted to be a part of the work, as if they are putting a part of themselves into the earthen works and plazas. When they finish an area of the plaza, they cover it with a good thick coat of a fine yellow silt, and it makes the plaza look golden. The Pilgrim has never seen anything so beautiful, a whole golden grand floor to walk across.

While the notion of abundant food and stability are appealing to a young man looking for an exciting new life, the Pilgrim sees opportunity for himself within a society and system in which he can prosper.

In his basket, the Pilgrim has his tribute crops that were ready for harvest, small ears of flint corn early planted, summer varieties of squash, ripe beans, and fresh fragrant greens of all types. The Pilgrim has timed his visit before the longest day of the summer, as he knows there will be a large ceremonial feast and he can help build a new mound and try to understand the complex planning of this great new city.

The Pilgrim marvels at the sheer size of the community neighborhoods along the way to the city center and the vastness of how far they extend. Thousands of people working in farming communities like his own, all living in tight little grass-thatched houses spread for hundreds of miles outside of the city center. Everywhere food being cooked, and the smell of hominy corn, roasted deer and elk, and corn and bean bread makes him hungry. Everyone seems to be in harmony in these early days, and the promise of food and learning fills the air with a simple happiness.

The Pilgrim takes his tribute crops to a large circular grass-thatched repository, which serves as a ticket of sorts to the ceremonial activities about to happen, and he is then given tools, a large stone hoe, and a basket to carry earth. The Pilgrim is told the way to his lodging for the festival, and he wanders the early evening, now cooling after the heat of the day. He wanders toward the city center and soon he sees throngs of workers carrying earth from borrow pits, men and women with hoes digging up certain colors of earth, some yellow, some red, and some a deep, dark black, all heading in different directions.

After taking his place in the long line of workers, he works up a sweat and feels he has contributed by the time the meal crews have finished their portions and the call to eat has come. The Pilgrim gladly puts down his tools and takes a plate of food. The Pilgrim feels elated *and is soon tossing the remains of his food and breaking his plate and throwing it inside the borrow pits, like everyone else. There is singing of songs that are new to him, and he quietly begins to hum along with the singers.*

Soon, he follows the throngs to the bigger mound plazas and watches as a ceremony, a sacred play, occurs on the main plaza and atop one of the largest mounds. The Pilgrim sees a man dressed as a Thunderbird and two elaborately dressed men, appearing to be twins, identically dressed in in blankets covered in shells and large, ornate headdresses with feathers and copper.

In the center of the platform atop the Great Mound, next to a House of the Dead, is a huge cypress tree, placed firmly into the earth of the platform. Magically to the crowd, two costumed Spirit Wolves appear from behind the massive Center Pole, meant to be the center of the known universe and a conduit from the Upper Realm above the clouds.[1]

The two Spirit Wolves descend the stairs of the Great Mound to the level of all who view the great play, but unbeknownst to the Spirit Wolves, around the corner of one of the sides of the Great Mound, a massive costumed Underwater Spirit in the form of a beaver waits, brutally capturing and ritually killing them, and dragging them back toward the swampy lands outside the Main Plaza, and then the torches at the base of the Great Mound go dark.

Torch lights burn again atop the Great Mound, and all eyes move back to the top of the platform of the Great Mound and to the Center Pole that has been adorned with branches by hidden hands, but this time, emerging from behind the Center Pole comes the figure of First Father, adorned with a great white plume. First Father is angry and paces, waiting and watching the stairs impatiently.

Finally, after a great while, he rushes down the great steps with his own torch into the darkness of the Lower Realm, where we see the torch of the Underwater Spirit is again rekindled, and he waits around the corner for First Father. When the two figures meet, they dance and mock fight, tempting one another with many passes and strikes. But the anger of First Father is apparent, his emotions betray him, and he makes a foolish move, and the obsidian dagger of the Underwater Spirit strikes First Father dead. The Underwater Spirit is triumphant and finishes off the act of ritually cutting off his head, holding the head with the great white plume, the symbol of First Father, in his hands, and the now ghostly headless body wanders back up the stairs and disappears behind the great Tree of Life.

In the next scene, three grand figures emerge from behind the great Tree of Life, led by the great Redhorn, with one braid colored with red ochre, long-nosed copper god maskette earrings, and an Otter turban on his head, with a great copper plate and an ogee symbol atop the turban. Redhorn is followed by two similarly dressed individuals, one man, one woman, draped in beautiful, adorned blankets with Thunderbird symbols made of shells sewn onto them. Each of the three has white paint adorning their bodies and stripes of red ochre painted vertically on their faces. They each carry sacred objects in each hand.

Solemnly, they descend the great stairs of the pyramid to the main plaza, where the actor in the Underwater Beaver Spirit costume waits for them, dagger in hand. Again, a great theater of war dancing commences, with the Beaver Water Spirit becoming tired, no match for the three of them, and then they are upon him, maces and spears ritually murdering the spirit.

Quietly triumphant, they gather the head of First Father, the great white plume of his office visible to all. As they advance up the stairs, their torches are extinguished halfway, to the gasps of the crowd, only to relight the torches, this time with a fourth figure, the now gloriously adorned First Father in all his finery of headdress and plumes, the mace of power in his hands. He is risen from the dead, and now he ascends back to the platform of the Great Mound, with his head *and soul attached, now he returns to the Upper Realm. All is whole again and balance and harmony are restored to the Upper and Lower Realms. All torch lights extinguish.*

Halfway up the stairs to the great pyramid, where the torches of Father, Son, and Grandchildren now extinguished, only to be relit, a torch lights again, and a costumed Grandmother Spider is seen to be weaving a great new web. The web of life of the Middle Realm. When Grandmother finishes her woven web, she arises from her work and darkness takes over the whole mound, and the crowd goes wild with cheering and much fanfare.

Thousands of people are there to watch the epic play. Ultimately, the Pilgrim finds a friendly face from his new farming community who tells him the story of First Father, the Earth Mother, and their many sons and the story of the Upper Realms and the Lower Realms, with their Thunderbirds and Underwater Serpents, and many epic battles with Giants. The friend whispers of the new star soon to be seen in the sky, the brightest of all stars, an omen, a time of great change in the universe.

The Pilgrim watches the sky expectantly, waiting for that new star, brighter than any other star, ushering in a new era, and waits for the new star to appear.

CAHOKIA 2017

My first adult glimpse of the Central Platform and the remnants of the once great Grand Plaza was bittersweet. Gone are the housing developments that remained when I was a child. In their place is a quaint visitor's center, neatly trimmed grass, and a maze of walking paths in and around the complex.

At its height, what lay before me was once over 200 earthen pyramidal works, or Mounds. This complex known as Cahokia was once a bustling, thriving mega center with a five-mile radius, a "city" whose population was greater than ten thousand. In the outlying "suburbs" were an additional twenty to thirty thousand people and farming communities within fifty miles in any direction.[2]

Henry Brackenridge, the first Euro-American to write about Cahokia, corresponded with former President Thomas Jefferson on the topic and wrote of his initial reaction:

> When I reached the foot of the principal mound, I was struck with a degree of astonishment, not unlike that which is experienced in contemplating the Egyptian Pyramids. What a stupendous pile of earth! . . . a very populous town had once existed here, similar to those of Mexico. . . . If the city of Philadelphia and its environs were deserted, there would not be more numerous traces of human bones.[3]

As I climbed the stairs up a vertical one hundred feet to the top of the Central Platform, I marveled at the gigantic endeavor it took to build this ancient earthen work. Its mass is over twenty-five million cubic feet and it covers almost fifteen acres. Standing at the top of the flat-topped geometric pyramid Mound, the wind blew sharply across my face as I scanned the jagged landscape dotted with a maze of smaller platform mounds that are strewn about in the Grand Plaza. Ironically, a view of downtown St. Louis looms in the background.

The Central Platform is the largest of the ancient earthen works on the North American continent, and the third largest in the Americas, surpassed only by the Pyramid of the Sun at Teotihuacan, just northeast of modern-day Mexico City.[4]

Situated just east of present-day East St. Louis, Illinois, the Cahokian Empire was a vast trading network extending its power from up north near Wisconsin, in the northern outpost known to anthropologists as Aztalan, down the Mississippi River Valley. The "old" city of Cahokia began around 700 CE, but by 1050, the "New Cahokia" began to explode in size and influence.

One of the most interesting questions regarding Cahokia is who built the Mounds. In his seminal work, *Cahokia: Ancient America's Great City on the Mississippi,* Timothy Pauketat has reworked through the history of Cahokia and the interconnected workings of the field of anthropology, melding the science of archaeology yet respecting the oral tradition of Indigenous peoples in a way that is propelling anthropology light-years into the future, away from its myopic and Eurocentric beginnings.

A key example of the debate is the iconic "Toltec Mounds" in central Arkansas, close to present-day Little Rock, Arkansas. Mrs. Gilbert Knapp, the owner of the land from the 1850s until the end of the century, aptly misnamed them and thought that the mystical Toltec race had brought the mound-building techniques from Mesoamerica,

Fig. 7.1. Cahokia. The Grand Mound and the Grand Plaza of Cahokia. While the true name of the mound complex and the individual names of each mound is not known, I prefer the more generic terms for some of them, like the Grand Mound, rather than "Monk's Mound" after some of the settlers who briefly inhabited it.

Photo courtesy of Taylor Keen

believing the ancestors of the modern-day Indigenous not capable of building the ancient earthen works.[5]

In the time between 700 to 1100 CE, the Toltec race of people and their entire central Arkansas River region was abandoned, and perhaps some of the Toltec took their traditions of mound building and certain burial practices up north into what would become Cahokia.

However, many anthropologists suggest that those people on the upper Missouri River were Caddoan (ancestors of the modern Pawnee and Arikara), based on comparative pottery fragments and styles.

As discussed in the companion chapter "The Founders' Dilemma of America: A First Peoples Historical Perspective of America," the prevailing attitude in the late 1800s of the burgeoning field of ethnology was a strong Eurocentric bias with respect to the Indigenous of America. John Wesley Powell, the Smithsonian's inaugural director, viewed the mounds as "vulgar curiosities," while many others in the field held the following opinion: "These mysterious Mound Builders, they thought, must have been wiped out by the later, warlike American Indians, or perhaps they migrated to Mexico to become the founders (sic) of the great civilizations of the Aztec and the Maya."[6]

The first voice in the camp of the "lost race of European Mound Builders" was a certain John Finch, who, when publishing a map of the Northwest Territory—above the area now known as Wisconsin—in 1785, placed the following inscription: This country has once been settled by a people more expert in the art of war than the present inhabitants. Regular fortifications, and some of these incredibly large, are frequently to be found. Also, many graves and towers like pyramids of earth.[7]

Even among those who did agree that the Indigenous races of North America were indeed the builders of the ancient earthen works, the question of who built which regions of the mounds were highly contested. Squier and Davis, the authors of the Smithsonian's first publication, *Ancient Monuments of the Mississippi Valley,* summarized the debate and their conclusions:

> We may venture to suggest that the facts thus far collected point to a connection more or less intimate between the race of the mounds and the semi-civilized (sic) nations which for many had their seats among the Sierras of Mexico, upon the plains of Central America and Peru, and who erected the imposing structures which from their number, vastness, and mysterious significance, invest the central portion of the continent with an interest not less absorbing than that which attaches to the valley of the Nile.[8]

Cyrus Thomas was appointed head of the Division of Mound Exploration by the Bureau of American Ethnology. Thomas's work was concluded with the publication of the Bureau's Annual Report of 1894. Initially, Thomas supported the position of the "lost race" theory.

Regardless, in the final version, Thomas's report slowly denounced much of the misinformation of the proponents of the "lost race" theory, stating: "That they are the work of Indians must be admitted by all who are willing to be convinced by evidence."[9]

THE BEGINNINGS OF THE MOUND BUILDERS

Some of the earliest earthen mound construction began around 3500 BCE in what is now northeastern Louisiana, where eleven earthen mounds were constructed in a large oval. Arguably, the builders were the people known by anthropologists as the Coles Creek Culture, from either eastern Siouan or Muskogean language speakers.

The Coles Creek Culture mounds were reminiscent of the southern Mesoamerican pyramid tradition, with flat-topped platform mounds in the middle of large ceremonial plazas, and they were likely were the templates for Cahokia. Archaeologists have found evidence of Cahokian-style pottery at Coles Creek locations and vice versa (see chapter 9, "Ten Thousand Years Ago and Beyond").

THE RISE OF THE CAHOKIAN EMPIRE

When we look at the term "civilization," it is typically defined by two broad activities, or rather, their intersection: mass agricultural production and a compelling religion. At Cahokia, you find agriculture and religion colliding, and the supernova of 1054 CE was the big bang catalyst to attract the masses.

The old city of Cahokia attracted new visitors and immigrants on a slow and steady basis. During the first millennium CE, local farmers began to toy with subtle variations in agronomy, such as different soil conditions, experimenting with planting densities, and rotating active and fallow fields.

By the 900s, corn had become the foundation of the growing populations at Cahokia, with a strong influx of immigrants to the area. At Cahokia's peak in the 1100s and 1200s, corn production had maximized, and there was a shift of population from the city center to the outskirt villages, illustrating the decentralized nature of agriculture versus the urban ceremonial focus.[10] The population of Cahokia at the city center grew from around fifteen hundred to over ten thousand, and by the 1100s and 1200s the population outside of the city center would be many more than at the city center. It's hard to imagine, but ancient Native Americans were fleeing from downtown to the suburbs.

But there was something more, something spectacular that happened one morning in the year 1054 CE. In the sky was seen a new star, four times brighter than Venus and visible to the naked eye during the night and day, hanging next to the crescent moon. And not just any new star, but a supernova. Today we know the supernova created the Crab Nebula, in the constellation of Taurus. Seen all around the globe, the event date was July 4, 1054, as noted by a Chinese astrologer.[11]

CAHOKIA CITY CENTER, SUMMER OF 1054

The Pilgrim is now calling himself Honga ("The one from whom we all descend"), after one of the heroes portrayed on top of the platform Mound that he witnessed when he first came to Cahokia. Honga was one of the Thunder Twins of the Sun, the first grandchildren of First Father and Mother Corn, the sons of Morningstar.

Honga was trying to focus on his first visit to the theater platform mound, trying to recall the saga he saw when he first arrived. This time, as he watched the pageantry in front of him, there were thousands more people to witness it, who had come when the bright new star had appeared in the sky, twice as bright as any other star and even visible during the day. The priests had said many people would come to see the story of First Father's ascension, and now they were here.

The saga of the Twins was his favorite part of the new religion he was learning at Cahokia. Honga was fascinated by the whole story of the First Family. He made sure to go through the story many times in his head, as he knew he would be asked to recount it for his home farming community.

Honga thought through the whole story and began reconstructing in his mind the story he had seen at the ceremony whenever he worked on the earthen works with his hands. It brought him a peace and a calm when he let his mind relax, and he would go over and over the story in his mind:

First Father was from the Upper Realm, where the Thunder Beings lived, their emissaries the Thunderbirds, whose home was the great cedar trees way in the West. In the earliest days, there was only the Upper Realm and the Lower Realm, with no Middle Realm, which is the realm we human beings occupy. The Sun and the skies belong to men, and thunder and fire are the working tools of the Thunder Beings and of men.

The Lower Realm was ruled by the Underwater Spirits, chief among them being the Underwater Panther, who ruled all the water spirits. The water, the moon, which is filled with the Water of Life, belongs to the spirit of Mother Corn, or First Mother, and all mothers. Some of our stories say the Creator made First Mother from a cob of corn planted in the Upper Realm.

First Father and First Mother's union in the Upper Realm produced ten sons and two daughters, Evening and Morning Star. One of these daughters gave birth to the Thunder Twins.

First Father was curious about the Lower Realm and sent two Spirit Wolves, his emissaries, down to explore on his behalf. The two Spirit Wolves were captured and eaten by a great Beaver Water Spirit, and First Father, enraged, foolishly went down to the Lower Realm to redeem his Spirit Wolves. Some say he gambled with the spirit for his agents, and some say they dueled. First Father lost the gamble, and the Beaver Water Spirit captured First Father's head but sent his lifeless body back to the Upper Realm, where it could never complete the Journey of the Souls back to its original dwelling place in the Seven Sisters constellation without the complete body intact.

First Father's grandsons, the Thunder Twins, sought to avenge the loss of First Father. They journeyed to the Lower Realm after a battle with the Giants, and they bested the Beaver Water Spirit and brought back the head of First Father so he could ascend to his celestial home and complete his Journey of the Souls.

This story and the ascension of First Father became the pilgrimage of all the souls here in the Middle Realm. The journey of First Father from the Upper Realm to the Lower Realm created a rift between the two realms, and Grandmother Spider wove our world with her silk.

This story is what Honga witnessed on one of the platform mounds on his first journey to the city center. Honga watched as each of these heroes was portrayed in a grand play for all to see. How revered would Honga be if he could portray First Father or one of his Twin saviors?

Through the salvation of First Father, each of us in the Middle Realm could find eternal salvation and ascension to the Upper Realm and our home among the stars.

THE CHUNKEY ROLLER

Honga wanted nothing more than to find a place in this bustling and exciting new world. Having found stability as a laborer in the construction of the Grand Plaza and many earthen works, Honga was becoming complacent, and he hated the notion that he could not be more.

Honga watched the great theatrical performances about First Father, Redhorn, and the Twins and wished he could be considered worthy to be asked to portray them. What deeds must he perform to become worthy of such a role? Honga was not born into the dynastic families in power, and he knew he must prove his skills and strength if he was to climb the hierarchy of this great empire.

Honga had learned to love the stories about Redhorn, Morningstar, and the Twins, and he sought to emulate them whenever possible. Redhorn had been described to be a great chunkey player, and now the game was becoming the royal game of the Cahokian Empire. The game of chunkey had been played back in his childhood home village, but he had never dreamed of the grandeur, pomp, and circumstance in which the game was played here. The Cahokian Empire managed the tournaments and had seemingly regulated all the playing, systematically disallowing any playing of the game outside of the royal courts and tournaments.

On the Grand Plaza were brilliant courts of hard stone covered with a fine sand that enabled the chunkey players to roll their magnificent wheel-like stones for long distances. The courts were designed to accommodate many an observer, and many wagers were placed, many times over.

Honga had always considered himself a good chunkey player, not only having a deft ability to roll a chunkey stone gracefully, but he was also fleet of foot and able to throw the chunkey stick at the stone with remarkable precision, sometimes from great distances. The lower tournaments were the only way to start, and he hoped to win key matches in a dramatic enough fashion for the upper tournament judges to qualify him for the invitational.

After a few awkward wins and a handful of losses, Honga knew he would have to try something explosive to win and get picked for the Royal Invitational. The lower tournament courts were not proper courts, just areas laid out and ground so bumpy that long, graceful rolls were impossible. Honga devised a strategy of quick, hard rolls so that his stone was difficult to hit. The other players did not like this strategy, but it did not violate any rules. Honga's counterstrategy for hitting the others' stones was to strike with his spear as quickly as possible. This was a bold strategy, for if he missed, the others could simply wait for his rolls, but not if he hit more quickly than they did. This controversial style of play made him many enemies, but victory was most often his.

In time, as Honga perfected his chunkey strategy and his skills became better, the judges from the Royal Invitational noticed his bold style of play and winning record. Honga was invited to the Royal Invitational and was given a beautiful new rolling stone and a copper dart. Honga had only seen those copper chunkey sticks used in the Royal Tournament. Honga knew that the other players would know his strategy by now, and he decided to switch his approach to one suitable for the hard and nearly perfect chunkey courts on the Grand Plaza.

The other players expected him to play his quick and aggressive

Fig. 7.2. The Chunkey Roller. A carving of an ancient Mississippian, portraying a figure playing the game called chunkey.
Wikimedia Commons

short-term game, and so they were surprised when Honga introduced a smooth, graceful, elongated rolling style, punctuated with deep contemplation before and after each roll. Similarly, his throwing style was patient and graceful; he waited for the stone to slow down, which caused him to make longer throws, but the slow stone enabled his strategy to succeed, and when it did, the crowds went wild.

Honga had become like Redhorn, the chunkey roller of old: patient and wise.

CAHOKIA IN TRANSITION 1100–1200

There is a strong argument that Cahokia was more than a city, that it was a trading empire. Whether it was trading copper from the Great

Lakes, obsidian from Mesoamerica, or marine shells from the East Coast, we see the formation of an early economy. The Mississippian cultures that built Cahokia also built upon the traditions of those who inspired them; innovations in art, architecture, cosmology, sport, religion, and agriculture dominated the legacy left to us by the great builders of Cahokia.

As with all great cultures, this was not enough—they wanted to leave a Cahokian legacy behind. Thus, the "big bang" of Cahokia began to spread up the Mississippi to present-day archaeological sites now known as the Eveland site in Illinois, Aztalan, and Trempealeau sites in Wisconsin, as well as across the Midwest and to the Southeast in sites such as Angel, Kincaid, Shiloh, Moundville, and Ocmulgee. Cosmologically speaking, we see the influences in their art and tribal cosmologies of Mother Corn, Redhorn, the Twins, Thunderbirds, and the Underwater Panther / Serpent.

Let us examine the enigmatic legacy of the Twins.

THE THUNDER TWINS, CHILDREN OF THE SUN

First Father and Corn Mother were the first Thunder Beings, and they came directly from the Upper Realm, made directly by the hands and breath of the Creator, Earth Maker. In those days, there were still Giants that lived in the lands, and at times, there was peace with them, but they were arrogant and impatient, believing they were as talented and gifted as the Thunder Beings themselves. Along with the Giants, the Little People lived in the same realm, and they were much revered as Medicine People. They were respected, and many were afraid of them because of their different manners and powers. In those days, the animals and the human beings all spoke the same language.

First Father and Mother Corn had ten sons and two daughters,

Morning Star and Evening Star. Some tribal stories tell that the Twins come from one of the two sisters, others say that they are the progeny of the youngest of the brothers, He-Who-Wear-Human-Head-Earrings, others call him He-Who-Is-Hit-With-Deer-Lungs.

As the youngest of the ten brothers, he is teased and harassed and must prove himself. He-Who-Is-Hit-With-Deer-Lungs must take every opportunity to prove his value to his siblings,

He soon finds it when he hears there is to be a race with the Giants, who should be much bigger and faster than the brothers, but the brothers take the challenge, hungry to win. And for most of the race, it appears that the larger Giants are much faster than the brothers, but when the Giants come around the last corner to the finish, they are shocked to see He-Who-Is-Hit-With-Deer-Lungs victorious, as he had medicine power to transform himself into a red arrow and shot past the Giants to win the race.

The Giants, defeated, are not practiced in losing and soon challenge the brothers to a more serious game of stickball, the "Little-Brother-of-War." It is a serious game, very difficult, and with dire outcomes for the losing side. Not only does the captain lose his life, but so does the entire losing team.

Again, He-Who-Is-Hit-With-Deer-Lungs shows remarkable prowess on the field, perhaps by his own gifts, perhaps by magic, and the ten brothers again claim victory, and all the Giants lose their lives but one, a red-haired Giantess who asks that He-Who-Is-Hit-With-Deer-Lungs take her as a wife, and he does take her as a second wife. The first wife that He-Who-Is-Hit-With-Deer-Lungs took was Woman-Who-Wore-A-White-Beaver-Skin-Wrap, an orphan who truly loved him and was loyal to him, even when jealous brothers perpetrated rumors of his death.

Soon after, the youngest of the ten sons reveals his identity to all, as he spits in his hands and rubs his ears, and little heads appear on his ears, and they mock any who show interest. Next, the youngest

Fig. 7.3. Herb Roe's artistic interpretation of the Mississippian soteriological
hero known as Redhorn, One Horn, and Without Horns
from the Siouan and Southeastern Ceremonial Complex.
Wikimedia Commons

*son spits on his hands and rubs his long braid, and it becomes covered
with red ochre, and thus the legend of Redhorn is born.*

*Redhorn tells them he is from the Upper Realm, one of the five
sons created by Earth Maker and sent to Earth to help redeem the
human beings. Soon, the two wives of Redhorn become heavy with
child, and thus the brothers / twins are born into this world.*

FIRST WOMAN, MOTHER CORN,
AND THE SACRED FEMININE

Acknowledging and understanding the role of the sacred feminine to my ancestors and in the tribal tradition is one of the most cherished gifts I received in this journey. I have written separately about rediscovering some of the sacred feminine articles for the Omaha tribe, but I want to discuss the role of Mother Corn in the Mississippian tradition and within the Cahokian complex.

I am indebted to the scholarship of anthropologists Tim Pauketat and Susan Alt, as their progressively intuitive and culturally sensitive research into the role of the sacred feminine has been invaluable, and their paper "The Emerald Acropolis: Elevating the Moon and Water in the Rise of Cahokia."

When I began this project, I was seeking to understand the economic and environmental factors related to the ancient past, and I have discovered so much in cultural and traditional experiences along the way.

Let us begin with several archaeological finds relating to the sacred feminine, the first being the BBB Motor site, named after the car dealership whose construction was the impetus for the archaeology dig. Just a couple of miles from the main complex at Cahokia, this site yielded data that placed it being settled around 900 CE and becoming by 1050 CE a centralized mortuary site, with lots of engraved pots, medicinal plants, crystals, and the residue of burned objects.[12]

But it was a carving that yielded the truth and power of this site. Thomas E. Emerson, PhD, found in the earth the remains of a red stone carving of a woman kneeling on the ground and holding a stone hoe that was digging into a serpent with a toothy, almost feline, smiling face. The serpent's body bifurcated into two gourd vines that grew up her back. A basket, perhaps for the bones of the deceased, was on her back. The older elder could be any Indigenous person's grandmother, with the years of experience painted on her face, the blind faith of connecting agriculture to the symbols of the serpent and a veneration of the past.

While she is known by many names—Mother Evening Star, Mother Moon, Spider Woman, Mother Corn, Snake Woman, and Earth Mother—she is the deity all Mississippian women venerated. Mother Corn is First Woman, Mother of All, and she is tied to both the moon and the underworld, where the serpent resides, and all powers to grow crops are attributed to her.

> Earth Mother is the mythological mother of all humans and vegetation. She is the womb from which all life originates and to which all life returns with death. She is a symbol of the cycle of life. . . . With her help, the "Earth-Serpent," symbol of death and the underworld, provides the agricultural crops that humans need. On her back the goddess carries the pack or sacred bundle that is the symbol of fertility . . . The pack may be symbolic of rain, fertility, the source of knowledge, and the power of deities. It may contain human bones or the souls of men and women in the process of being returned to the land of the living. It may also contain the first seeds of the plants . . . given by Earth Mother to the People.[13]

From the same site, we have another feminine figurine rediscovered by the Emerson team. Here, we have a younger woman, also kneeling, with a basket in front of her this time and a plant in her hand. Perhaps as a younger persona, Mother Corn's basket is not for the bones of her ancestors, but for harvesting corn or perhaps it is for the Green Corn Ceremonies. I ponder if the figurine was utilized in instruction of how younger women were to act and to teach them what is important. I wonder if there is a connection between the corn itself and the ancestors, which is why the basket carries them both.

The Keller Figurine is another version of Mother Corn from the sphere of Cahokia. Most likely it was broken on purpose as a part of a burial or for a ceremonial use. The platform may be representing corn as she kneels next to a box like structure, perhaps a receptacle for agricultural seeds as Mother Corn is the connection between the sacred feminine and agriculture.

Finally, we come to the Halliday site, ten miles southeast of Cahokia, approximately a day's walk away. A small village was discovered at the site, consisting of about 150 homes and storage sheds. It was typical of the archaeological style, until they began to examine the types of pottery and other artifacts. The pottery styles were either foreign or old-fashioned, but more importantly, they seemed to have a whole different focus—no longer were the objects male-oriented, such as Redhorn, the Twins, Thunderbirds, or even hunting themes; now, they were feminine.

The archaeological team found weaving and yarn spindles and all sorts of implements to farm, cook, and make pottery. The inhabitants primarily ate corn and small animals. And they appear to be one of the farming satellite villages that produced an agricultural surplus for Cahokia. Archaeologists Pauketat and Alt believe these peoples, who began to migrate away from Cahokia around 1150 CE, might be ancestors of some of the southern Dhegihan Osage and Quapaw, as well as the Pawnee. Perhaps this was the beginning of the end of the Cahokian Empire? And the question remains: Why?

CAHOKIA 1075: THE CONQUERING WARRIOR AND THE PASSING OF THE THUNDER TWINS

Honga, after establishing his reputation as an excellent and graceful chunkey player and victor, decides it is time to leverage his momentum as an athlete and pursue a long-term path for himself within the Empire.

The Elite Guard of Cahokia were instantly recognizable by their attire: thick leather skullcap, big, circular ear spools made of flint clay, leather arm and leg bands, some with copper bracelets adorning the leather, a large leather backpack, and a flowing breechclout of individual strips of buckskin. Most of the Elite Guard of Cahokia carried the instrument of their office—a thick stick used for bludgeoning on one side and a razor-sharp copper alloy for a blade on the other.

They were known to be merciless, putting down insurgents within the empire, and were responsible for capturing woman for ritualized sacrifices from the suburban villages that paid tribute to the central Empire. Although he had never actually seen it, it was rumored that there were times when hundreds of people would be sacrificed if someone especially important in the Empire passed on to the Journey of the Souls.

In the case of the Grand Chief's passing, his female relatives would sacrifice themselves to go along with the Grand Chief when he would become a star; perhaps they would become stars themselves. Honga knew the grim reality that if they did not sacrifice themselves, the next dynasty of the incumbent Grand Chief would probably have them killed to avoid any question of his inheritance to be the clear ruler. The entirety of the family would typically be interred in a large earthen work constructed by everyone in the Empire, to pay respect.

Honga was on the official burial honor guard unit dispatched by the Grand Chief when the two Twins, who had been lauded as the reincarnation of the original Thunder Twins, passed from this realm and needed to make the Journey of the Souls. The Twins were revered and worshipped and always portrayed the original Twins in any of the royal theatrical productions. The Twins were royalty, as they were believed to be a reincarnation of the original Twins, the Grandsons of First Father and Earth Mother, or Mother Corn. This reincarnation of the twins found them to be both masculine and feminine, male and female.

To join them on the journey, most their female relatives had volunteered to sacrifice their lives here in the Middle Realm on behalf of the Twins. Clanship and thus societal identity were passed on by one's maternal line. Honga was moved by the great traditions of Cahokia and the blind faith that the loyal elite families had for the Empire. But as a part of the Cahokian guard, he knew what would happen to them once the Twins were gone and a new set of twins were picked to be the next generation.

The passing of the Twins was met with much grieving, pomp, and circumstance. The Twins were buried in the same mound, one meant to convey the passing of one era to another, noted in the movements of our planet to the constellations of the star. The Priests kept up with those meticulous movements in time, but Honga knew the Priests had expected the timing of their deaths. Their bodies were interred in the mound in a unique fashion: one was buried face up, and beneath him the other Twin was buried face down, to commemorate the duality of the Upper Realm and the Lower Realm. Between them and around them, tens of thousands of shells had been poured into their funerary bed in the shape of a Thunderbird to escort them on their journey. Elaborate blankets with Thunderbirds of shells and feathers covered their bodies at Mound 72 at Cahokia.

Honga, without emotion, approached one of the women surrounding the grave site and, without hesitation, took her life so she could join her relatives, the Twins.

Honga was beginning to understand how tenuous the careful balance of the Empire was. The stories of Redhorn were retold before the annual Morningstar Ceremony, where it was said that Redhorn himself had said that the people of the Empire must sacrifice a captive woman. The Empire must ensure the sacrifice for the blessings of Redhorn to continue in the Empire. Honga knew that many people were beginning to wonder if that were true, for it was terrible for those families that had to make the sacrifices. But these sacrifices

Fig. 7.4. Conquering Warrior Effigy Pipe, through to be from CE 1100–1200. Made of flint clay, it was found in Le Flore County, Oklahoma, at the Spiro site, Craig Mound.
Wikimedia Commons

kept order in the Empire, he was trained by the Elite Guard teachings to understand. The Elite Guard kept order in the Empire. Someone had to do it, and if he were going to continue to rise in the Empire, then he must do his work diligently.

THE MYSTIC CAHOKIA 1085: THE MYSTIC INITIATE

Honga was good at his work as a captain in the Elite Guard of Cahokia; he followed orders well, showed respect to his superiors, and was merciful to his victims of sacrifice or offering by being quick with his mace or his blade. None suffered but a quick and powerful blow.

But Honga was becoming numb toward his work. He longed to put this type of work behind him, and he sought contemplation more and more. Some of the members of the Elite Guard had gone on to become initiates of the Grand Medicine Lodge, and they were the only ones who seemed to be at peace after a long stint in the Elite Guard of Cahokia.

Honga began to ask some of the former Elite Guard members who had joined the Grand Medicine Lodge about the requirements of gaining entry. It was much more philosophical and introspective than he had imagined. Honga began preparing his gifts to be given to each of the Chiefs who occupied various important positions in the pantheon.

When Honga's gifts were finally ready after many months, he arrived at the thatched roof building where the other initiates were lining up in front of him. Each of them carried the bundle of gifts in a basket, and they were naked save a breechclout, and their hair pulled into a bun with purple flint clay spools in their ears.

Soon, the initiates were kneeling in the Teaching Lodge, a clay cup with designs of the empire on the side and a curious black drink in front of them. Honga knew this black drink was medicine, and it tasted both bitter and sour, and he drank deeply and listened to the songs being sung, and slowly his mind began to focus and open, and he kept his eyes closed and meditated on the songs and the medicine working on him, and he soon began to dream, a waking dream . . .[14]

Fig. 7.5. The Mystic Initiate. This carving from the Spiro Mounds (not from a burial) shows a figure kneeling in apparent reverence and in prayer or awaiting instruction. These types of figures are often associated with the "Black Drink," which may have been a purgative or a psychedelic, allowing for purification and/or enhanced dreams of visions.
Wikimedia Commons

THE CAHOKIAN DECLINE 1200–1350 CE

Honga V, fifth-generation political dynastic Chief, sits adorned in full regalia upon his throne atop his mound, the one they will bury him in when it is his time to complete his Journey of the Soul. The massive headdress alone, filled with feathers from all the four directions and as colorful as any rainbow, is a tribute to how much he has grown the empire and its vast trading network.

Honga held in his hand the copper chunkey dart that his ancestor, Honga I, won many years ago in the famed heyday of the Royal Invitational Chunkey Tournament finals. It was Honga's chosen symbol of his power and office. He admired the brilliant hue of the copper, unmatched anywhere in the world, from the great lakes to the north. A bittersweet token, as one of his greatest disappointments was the failure of those outposts, which were directly north on the river out of Cahokia.

Honga had hoped that the Algonquins would have been strong allies, partners in the riches of the copper mines and keepers of stories like the ones told at Cahokia, an homage to the great Tree of Life and the Upper and the Lower Realm. Honga had long admired their ability to tell stories in their earthen work effigy constructions. But it was not to be. At first, they traded with the Cahokians, but they solemnly rejected his offers of diplomacy.

But as time went on, the Algonquin not only rejected diplomacy, but they also retaliated. The few surviving messengers who escaped told horrific stories of burning palisades and full-scale calculated attacks on multiple outposts.

Honga had then turned his attention to matters of home. The supplies of crop tribute had been waning for some time, but now they had become erratic. There was not enough food to feed all his citizens. Over the generations of his family's dynasty, the huge cypress trees that had been used to build the Great Woodhenge had become all but extinct. The zealous growth of the Empire had ravaged and transformed the shoreline of the great river until it was nearly devoid of trees, and the river was taking over, widening and changing course easily in a heavy rainy season. Honga worried that a major deluge would flood even the city center itself.

Also, Honga's advisors were torn about building a bastion wall around the city center. The debates were wide and varied: some argued that the single authority of his family's dynasty was losing its favor with the Morningstar deity and those gods appointed by Earthmaker himself to help the humans, and therefore, the city was becoming vulnerable.

Some of Honga's other advisors commented that the citizenry of Cahokia no longer looked to the city center and the Elite Guard to officiate, even at burials, and they no longer needed the Priests to pray for them and make their offerings because they were now doing it themselves.

Yet other advisors wanted to build the bastion walls to effectively keep people in. Honga scoffed at this notion, and when the other Elite Guards had spoken their minds, Honga called the meeting complete and told everyone to leave to let him think.

Slowly, the outlying communities were in exodus. Honga trusted his advisors, who told him to increase the number of sacrifices to the spirit of Morningstar, that the bloodlust of the people yearned for it. Honga did know that the sacrifices were critical in keeping tension in the outlying communities, for the loyal families were never chosen to give up one of their own for a sacrifice. But perhaps the sway of his empire was waning, and the opposite effect was starting to happen: the sacrifices were driving them away from the empire.

Honga wondered why they stayed; after all, what did they receive for their crop tribute? Administration from the priests? An occasional communal feast? There was a time, he was told through his father and grandfather, when simply working together on the Mounds brought *energy and healing. The pilgrims had come from long and far away to be a part of that energy. Honga wished dolefully that he could have felt and seen that kind of energy. Now, it felt like everything was forced, that the Priests doubted his ability to commune with Earthmaker, and his wife's ability to invoke Earth Mother and the great Serpent in the Lower Realm.*

Honga sighed and knew his answer: he ordered the building of the bastion walls.

CAHOKIA, EPILOGUE

By around 1200, most anthropologists agree, there was a decline at Cahokia, and by 1350–1400, it was all but abandoned. Typical theories of the reason for the decline of the Cahokian civilization range from political upheaval of the caste system, systemic climate change, deforestation impacts, overfarming, drought, war, plague, and even, now, flooding.

Sam Muñoz and Jack Williams, two geographers at the University of Wisconsin, published a work in the Proceedings of the National Academy of Sciences, which illustrates that the rise of Cahokia took place during a period uncharacteristically devoid of flooding, but sediment coring has proven that there was a large flood around approximately 1200 that left the soil without pollen. And without pollen, you have no plants. This event could have likely worked in concert with the other factors in the city's decline and eventual abandonment.

Archaeologist Tim Pauketat has a theory regarding "redistributing ideology" and "tribute crops" that allowed the central empire of Cahokia to appropriate a tax on communal items such as crops, so a pilgrim or a newcomer to Cahokia could proverbially pay their entrance fee into the society. What did they get in return? Access to the cosmological stories referenced earlier in the chapter. Innovation and new ideas are always appreciated in any time or era, and I wonder if there were not enough new stories to attract migrating pilgrims to Cahokia and retain them. Couple that with flood and drought and a loss of food supply, and the Cahokia's whole economic model is in jeopardy. And, for certain, the disregard for the sanctity of life involved in the human sacrifices sanctioned by the city state of Cahokia would eventually cause a backlash, if not an outright revolt. In our oral traditions, the Cherokee share this last sentiment—that eventually we fought the priestly caste system and revolted. Tyranny is never a long-lasting strategy for any society.

AS ABOVE, SO BELOW

*Archaeoastronomy of the Earthen Works and
the Journey of the Souls*

INTRODUCTION: WHAT ARE THE MOUNDS AND WHAT DO THEY REPRESENT SYMBOLICALLY?

My journey into the ancient earthen works began with Cahokia (see the preface and chapter 7), but soon the entirety of up to ten thousand of these earthen mound complexes that once lay across the Ohio River Valley slowly revealed themselves to me like solemn witnesses to a larger truth that I have never imagined. The question is always the same: What was their purpose and why did they exist?

The first question is are they burial mounds? Yes, many of them are for burial purposes, but others could have marked important places of sacred geography or even been route or territorial markers. Some of the earthen works might have been in proximity to special plants, minerals, or medicines. Some earthen works were for healing or vision questing or to connect with the spirit world. Many earthen works were for rituals and ceremonies. Still others were meeting places for social, political, and economic activities, such as trade. I will argue later in this chapter that many were part of a religious pilgrimage to marry heaven with earth, and that many of the mounds were for purposes of archaeoastronomy.

Who built them? Many of the earthen works across the Ohio River

ANCIENT WORKS, MARIETTA, OHIO.

Fig. 8.1. Marietta Works. This illustration by gives readers a glimpse of what
this site may have looked like in antiquity.
Squier and Davis, *Ancient Monuments of the Mississippi Valley,* 1848

Valley were from the Adena and the Hopewell cultures. These names
are anthropological and archaeological terms and, from the Indigenous
perspective, are antiseptic and impersonal, focusing from a Eurocentric
perspective on the anthropologists or landowners who "discovered"
them. Regardless, they give us classification of common themes, methodologies, and motifs.

The Adena cultural period begins somewhere between 800 and
500 BCE and ends around 100 CE. The landscape boundaries of the
Adena were southern Ohio, southeastern Indiana, northern and central
Kentucky, West Virginia, and southwestern Pennsylvania. One of the
notable attributes of Adena earthen works is the incorporation of burial
mounds, and many of them are conical in nature.

In those earthen works that are burial mounds, there is usually more than one individual interred, and often the burials are in wooden or stone tombs with earthen layers built up over them. At times, the earthen mounds were used to cover circular wooden structures, which may have been ceremonial sites situated over sacred geography. Another trademark of the Adena works are the incorporation of sacred circles—raised earthen circles with an interior ditch. Artifacts found within the Adena works range from tubular pipes to various styles of gorget, and copper bracelets.

The Hopewell cultural period picked up from the end of the Adena period around 100 CE and lasted until around 400 CE. The Hopewell works are potentially an extension of the Adena works, although they could be separate cultural groups who simply were inspired by the design and cosmology of the Adena. Hopewellian earthen works are larger, and in some cases, more complicated in design.

The types of artifacts found in the Hopewell earthen works include rocker-stamped pottery, ritual smoking pipes, large cymbal-shaped ear spools, obsidian points, and mica cutouts. Even the materials utilized to create these objects became more elaborate, such as copper, silver, gold, meteoric iron, mica, crystal quartz, animal teeth, and even freshwater pearls. Most likely these more exotic materials came from an enhanced trading network.[1]

One definition of archaeoastronomy is the study of how people in the past "have understood the phenomena in the sky, how they used these phenomena and what role the sky played in their cultures," says Rolf M. Sinclair, founding member and chair emeritus of the Inspiration of Astronomical Phenomena (INSAP) and author of *Current Studies in Archaeoastronomy: Conversations Across Space and Time.*

But with respect to the ancient Mississippian earthen works, the preemptive authority is William F. Romain, PhD, an archaeologist who specializes in the study of ancient religions, cognitive archaeology, and archaeoastronomy. Romain brought the technology of lidar (light detection and ranging) to the Mississippian earthen works, specifically to the Great Serpent Mound in Adams County, Ohio. Among technologies Romain and his team employed to analyze the earthen works were geoprobe coring, hand coring, limited excavation techniques, ground-penetrating radar, and electric resistivity analysis.

Romain has given us much with his work on the Great Serpent Mound, and by examining his writing in some detail, I can show you some of the deeper complexities of the earthen works. In his latest work, *An Archaeology of the Sacred: Adena-Hopewell Astronomy and Landscape Archaeology,* Romain argues for a deeper understanding of Adena-Hopewell culture:

Adena-Hopewell religion comprised cultural-level cosmological understandings integrated with actor-based perceptual experiences, that, together, inform a characteristic Adena-Hopewell way of being-in-the-world. This way of being-in-the-world emerged as a relational field that entangled individual sensory experiences and interactions with a variety of non-human agents and forces, cosmic realms, and numinous earth, sky, and water phenomena.[2]

Romain continues in his explanation that "relational fields can entangle all manner of actors to include gods, angels, demons, ghosts, spirits, souls of the living as well as the dead . . . non-human agents can include plants, animals, sun, moon, stars, mountains, lakes, rivers, and other earth, sky, and water, things, as well as the earthworks and mounds themselves."

Let's explore some of the concepts you read in chapter 7, "Cahokia." The characters of Honga and Morningstar find their place in a Cahokian society, playing a role in a larger communal society. By working in the fields or on earthwork construction, both find a place alongside living heroes, living constructs of earth, and the ghosts of Redhorn, First Father, and Earth Mother. The spirit of Redhorn is grotesquely honored through the sacrifices of the Conquering Warrior, and the Lower Realm spirit is invoked by women as they plant.

To Romain, the Upper Realm, the Lower Realm, and the Middle World (ours) is a cosmological concept of a "vertically tiered cosmos," and the vertical axis mundi that connects those worlds. In my opinion, the axis mundi is the Tree of Life. Additionally, Romain establishes a concept he refers to as "hierophanies" or places that can be "experienced in transcendental ways, beyond common experiences." In terms of the earthworks, "By physically situating monumental earthworks in sacred time-space places or constructing earthworks that themselves created sacred time-space place . . . facilitated access to the world of spirit."[3]

At places like Cahokia and specifically at the Great Serpent Mound, we have sacred spaces that allow the participant to connect with the tiered realms of the universe, where the Upper Realm and Lower Realms are accessible in our space here in the middle realms.

But before we dive in too deep, let us examine some of the rudimentary aspects of the earthen works. Many of the earthen works are either mathematical-shape mounds or effigy mounds. The mathematical-shape mounds could be as simple as the work below:

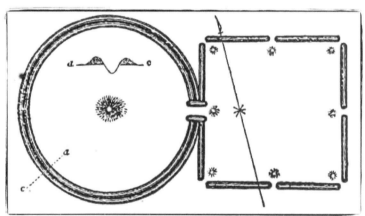

Fig. 8.2. The Circleville Mound demonstrates the basics mound building concepts of a circle and a square, equal in area and perimeter, exemplifying sacred geography and sacred geometry.
Squier and Davis, *Ancient Monuments of the Mississippi Valley*, 1848

Here we have an earthwork known as the Circleville Mound, and it is two seemingly simple mathematical earthworks, a circle and a square. The circle is unique in that it is two concentric walls with a ditch in between them. The outer circle is 1,140 feet in diameter and has an opening passage where the circle meets the square enclosure, whose sides measure 908 feet. The walls of the square were at least 5–6 feet high (in the 1840s, when Squier and Davis measured them, they felt erosion had taken much of the height by the time they surveyed them).

Another aspect to this plain mathematical work is that from a purely geometric perspective, we see a concept defined as "squaring the circle," where the two shapes are "unified by being made equal in area or perimeter . . . so that Heaven and Earth, or Spirit or Matter, are symbolically combined, or married."[4]

Not only is the Circleville Mound beautiful in terms of its mathematical precision, but the shapes are symbolic not only of Heaven and Earth, but also of the sacred masculine and feminine.

The circular work with a mound precisely in its center is a sun symbol and is masculine in most Indigenous cosmologies. "Point within a circle" is known for being the alchemical symbol for gold, the Egyptian symbol for the sun god Ra, and the Monad or the Absolute to the Pythagoreans.

The square in the abovementioned earthen work of Circleville has eight circular clay mounds inside the perimeter walls, symbolic of the eight phases of the moon.

THE MARIETTA EARTHEN WORKS

Another iconic and beautifully simple earthen works is the Marietta Mounds, a National Historic Site in Marietta, Ohio. One of the few fully intact works left, it is situated on an elevated plain on the banks of the Muskingum River at its confluence with the Ohio River.

The earthworks are comprised of two large, square earthen enclosures. The larger measures approximately 50 acres and includes four raised platform mounds, the larger two of which are referred to as the Quadranaou Mound and the Capitolium Mound.

Parallel and adjacent to the large, square opening that led to the Muskingum River lies a structured pathway often referred to as the Sacred Via, which was most likely a ceremonial passage to the water for water purification purposes.

The second square enclosure is smaller at 27 acres but with eight smaller mounds placed near the gaps between the earthen walls. This construction is like the square at Circleville mentioned above, and it most likely served as a lunar marker.[5]

Parallel and adjacent to the smaller of the square enclosures is the Conus Mound. Despite being covered by urban sprawl, all five mounds of this earthen work still survive today.[6]

Archaeologist William Romain proved that a cliff on the other side of the river could be sighted through small conical mounds, which would allow the viewer to stand on the Sacred Via at sunset on the winter solstice and watch the setting sun coming down to a point on the cliff that is across the river and in alignment with the Sacred Via.[7]

As we examine a magnification of the side elevations of the Marietta Earthen Works, we again see a level of algebraic precision and asymmetric symmetry.

The Sacred Via was a physical representation of the celebration of the sanctity of water, most likely designed to host a multitude of water blessings and ceremonies on the Muskingum River.

On the larger map, look to the most southern work, the circular mound. This mound is referred to commonly as the Conus Mound. It is important, for it is theorized to be an axis mundi symbol (center of the universe) and is strategically placed "at the intersection of the summer solstice sunrise and summer solstice sunset sightlines."

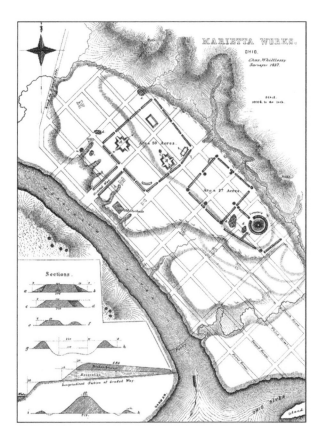

Fig. 8.3a. Ancient Works, Marietta, Ohio. The topographical illustration of the Marietta Works demonstrates the capacities of ancient Indigenous peoples for civil engineering, public planning, architecture, and construction.
Squier and Davis, *Ancient Monuments of the Mississippi Valley*, 1848

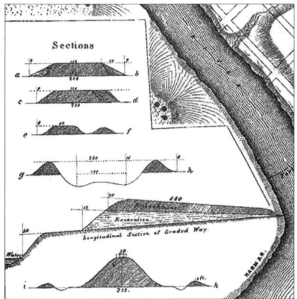

Fig. 8.3b. Side Elevation Marietta Works. This side elevation of the Marietta Works not only demonstrates precise building, but graphically exemplifies the sacred geometry and algebra of this ancient site.
I am reminded of mathematical models, such as sine and cosine.
Squier and Davis, *Ancient Monuments of the Mississippi Valley*, 1848

Based on the standardized Hopewell Measurement Unit (1,054 feet) and variations of that length and based in square, it can be assessed that the rest of the complex is laid out "orientated to the winter solstice sunset."

Romain further theorized that the Conus Mound was a holdover from the previous Adena Phase and that, while the rest of the earthworks at Marietta are Hopewellian, this site incorporates characteristics of both phases. Romain considers the Capitolium Mound to be of the Hopewell Phase but astronomically tied to the Conus Mound along a solstice alignment.

In summary, the individual mounds of the Marietta Works, the axis mundi of the Conus Mound, and subsequent alignments to the other mounds sited to witness solar solstices define an homage to the Sky. The Sacred Via with its ornate design is oriented to the sanctity of the sun, while yet remaining a path leading to water. And the earthen works themselves are of the earth. Here we have an "intersection of earth, sky and water realms."[8] A trinity of beauty.

Below is the iconic illustration from the Squier and Davis work *Ancient Monuments of the Mississippi Valley.*

Fig. 8.4. Great Mound at Marietta, Ohio. The Great Mound at Marietta is perfectly conical, with an adjacent ring that is reminiscent of a perfect sphere being dropped in water with the resulting ripple.

Squier and Davis, *Ancient Monuments of the Mississippi Valley*, 1848

THE PORTSMOUTH EARTHEN WORKS

Situated at the confluence of the Scioto and Ohio Rivers, the Portsmouth Earthworks is a set of four mound groups: Group A Old Fort, Group B the Citadel, Group C Temple Mound, and Group D Biggs Mound.

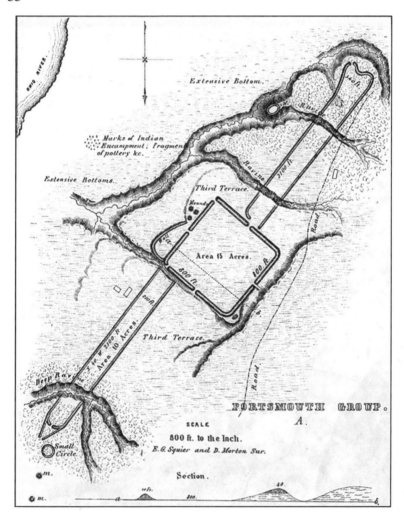

Fig. 8.5a. Portsmouth Works, Group A. "The Old Fort" at Portsmouth may be a ceremonial complex with the oblong mounds being aligned to the winter solstice sunrise, comprising the Hopewell Measurement Unit.

Squier and Davis, *Ancient Monuments of the Mississippi Valley*, 1848

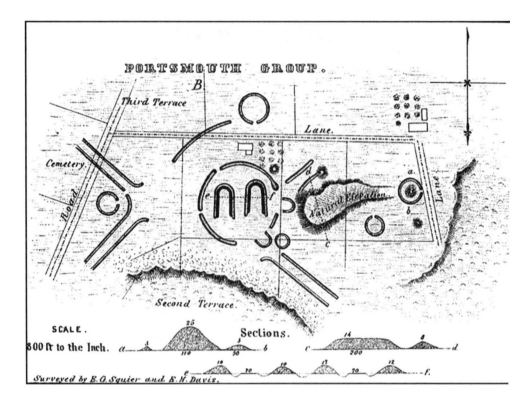

Fig. 8.5b. Portsmouth Works, Group B. The Citadel at the Portsmouth
Works, before obliteration by settlers, with a series of U-shaped mounds,
reflecting tribal notions of moon reverence and probable ceremonies by
tribal peoples to witness the movements of the moon.
Squier and Davis, *Ancient Monuments of the Mississippi Valley*, 1848

Group A's Old Fort is a square aligned "to both earth and sky" in
which the winter solstice sunrise can be viewed in the "minor axis of the
square." An east-to-west diagonal of the square is equal to 1,054 feet, or
one HMU (Hopewell Measurement Unit).[9]

The second group, or the Citadel, is a complex set of earthen works,
now mostly obliterated, but containing a pronounced circle enclosing a
series of U-shaped works, which, if observing the moon, one will find
that the maximum moon north rise and maximum moon north set.[10] I
believe this to be an aspect of tribal moon reverence and that ceremonies would have taken place here.

THE SERPENT EARTHEN WORKS

Finally, we have the Temple Mound or Group C. Notice the serpent-shaped design of the "Ancient Lines" and "Lines of Embankment" leading to the Citadel from the east and west, where they terminate at the Temple Mound.

The Temple Mound is situated on the Kentucky side of the Ohio River, some four miles south of the city of Portsmouth. At the time of Squier and Davis's original survey work, the Temple Mound was at the bend of the river, and this is still the case today, although the Ohio has changed course since then. The reader might remember that the sacred geography surrounding Pahuk was also a major, serpentine bend of the

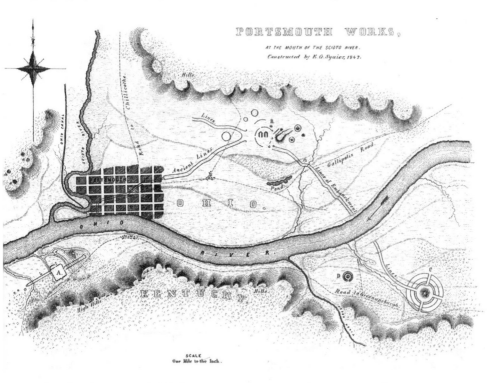

Fig. 8.6. Portsmouth Works, Group C. The Temple or Serpent Mound at Portsmouth is one of the most tantalizing mound complexes with its serpentine design connecting it to the Citadel.
Squier and Davis, *Ancient Monuments of the Mississippi Valley*, 1848

river. Perhaps the sacred aspects of the Temple Mound is its circular geography, combined with the ritual use of the Temple as a factor in the adoration of water as a part of recognizing and celebrating the sacred feminine?

In terms of design and form, Temple Mound sits at the center and is surrounded by concentric circular walled embankments, although, sadly, today it is not visible at the ground level. We hope to soon have lidar data available.[11]

Note the comparison to another similar serpent-like earthen works, this time at Avebury in Wiltshire, England, seventeen miles north of Stonehenge. Inside a great circle, which still stands, there was once a "serpent temple," as sketched by the British antiquarian William Stukeley in 1724. It could be assumed that a serpent passing through a circle would be alchemical in nature.

The serpentine works appear to be very similar, although thousands of miles away from each other and across the Atlantic Ocean. Are they connected? Or is it coincidence?

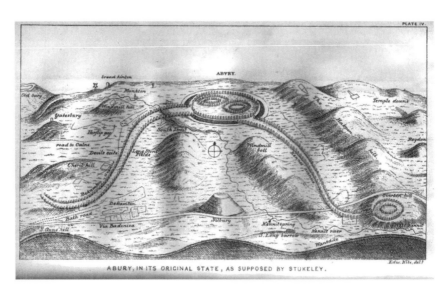

Fig. 8.7. Avebury Serpent Mound. The Avebury Temple and stone monument was erected 2,000 BCE is more than like the Portsmouth Temple Mound, with its serpentine nature, yet with solar aspects.
Stuckley, *Abury, A Temple of the British Druids, With Some Others, Described*, 1743

There is one fundamental difference between them: the Avebury stonework has a head on the end of the section to the right (fig. 8.7).

The difference with the terminus on the Portsmouth work is self-evident. It is more than a circle; it is a centered conical mound and then a series of concentric circular embankments and ditches surrounded by four perpendicular passages, one to each of the cardinal directions, with one connecting with the serpentine or "embankment line."

We covered this interesting terminus in chapter 2, "An Island in the East."

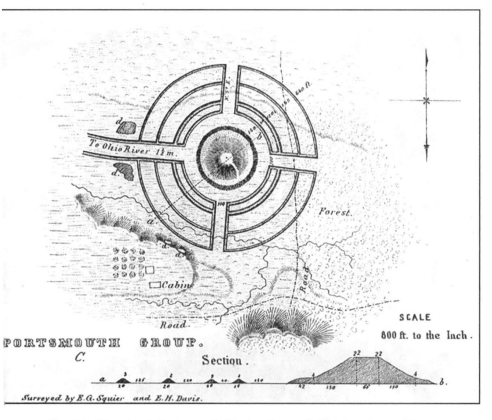

Fig. 8.8. (Terminus) Portsmouth Works, Group C. The terminus of the Temple Mound complex at Portsmouth, strikingly like Plato's description of Atlantis, but also like other Hopewellian circular enclosures with centrally located burial mounds.
Squier and Davis, *Ancient Monuments of the Mississippi Valley*, 1848

Finally, we come to the grandest of the serpentine mounds, the Great Serpent Mound of Ohio.

THE GREAT SERPENT MOUND OF OHIO

The Great Serpent Mound is indeed majestic: the body three undulating serpentine coils, curving ever so softly, its tail fully coiled into a spiral, and the head with its mouth agape, trying to engulf its prey, an oval. The entire design is arched and about to fully uncoil as it strikes its prey.

From a design aesthetic alone, the form rivals the Great Pyramid of Giza (completed around 2560 BCE), the Sphinx of Giza (perhaps built during the Khafre dynasty, 2558–2532 BCE), or the Parthenon of Greece (completed around 483 BCE).

If fully uncoiled, its length would reach almost a quarter of a mile. The height ranges from under a foot at the tip of the tail to a few feet at the head. Located in Adams County in western Ohio, close to the Ohio River, the Great Serpent Mound sits on an elevated plateau overlooking Brush Creek.[12]

How old is Serpent Mound? While debated in many academic circles, the original thinking was the Great Serpent Mound was attributed to the Adena culture approximately 800 BCE to CE 100. However, recent radiocarbon dating found the age of the Great Serpent ranges from a conservative estimate of 920 years BP plus or minus 70 years BP, based on various carbon dating techniques.

In 1996, archaeologists Robert Fletcher and Terry Cameron reopened a trench created by F. W. Putnam over one hundred years prior and extracted two pieces of charcoal that were both radiocarbon dated to approximately 1070 CE (900 years BP) and a third piece dating to slightly earlier.[13]

Finally, the carbon dating dilemma was reconciled by a team led by William Romain, which found much older charcoal samples in the less

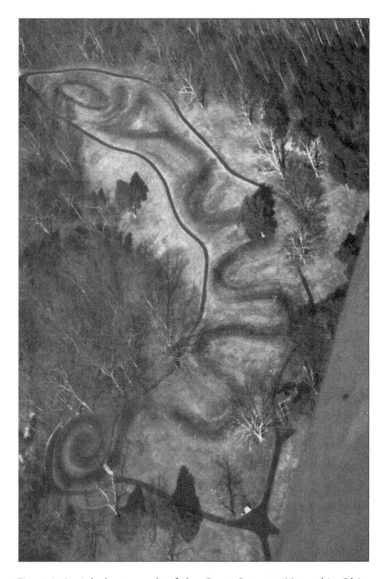

Fig. 8.9. Aerial photograph of the Great Serpent Mound in Ohio.
From *Star Mounds: A Legacy of a Native American Mystery* by Ross Hamilton.
North Atlantic Books, 2012. Courtesy of Ross Hamilton.

damaged areas of the mound, leading the team to find a range of 320 BCE, during the Early Woodland period, over two thousand years ago. The team also inferred that the later 1070 CE might have been a repair to the older site, thus corresponding to the earlier carbon dating dates.[14]

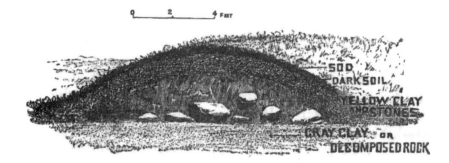

Fig. 8.10. F. W. Putnam's cross-section diagram detailing the
constitution of the mound's construction.

From *The Mystery of the Serpent Mound: In Search of the Alphabet of the Gods* by Ross
Hamilton. Frog Books, 2001. Courtesy of Ross Hamilton.

It is based on the inferences of F. W. Putnam and his cross-section
diagram, which hypothesizes that the Great Serpent was constructed
of a foundation of gray/rock clay, then the main "body" of the effigy
was made of a yellow clay reinforced with rocks, and finally, a humus
or topsoil accumulated naturally on top of both of those strata over a
very long period.

The Great Serpent Mound is beautiful in its design, but it is so
much more. It has deep cosmological foundations and incorporates
divine proportions and archaeoastronomy.

The Serpent Mound was first rediscovered in modern times by
Squier and Davis and described in their *Ancient Monuments of the
Mississippi Valley* in 1848, but then championed in the late 1880s by
F. W. Putnam, who is credited with saving the site as well as garner-
ing the spoils of its contents. Putnam ensured the safety of the Serpent
Mound by donating the park to the Ohio Historical Society, but at
the same time, like many antiquarians of the day, ensured that most of
the contents inside the Serpent Mound made their way to the Peabody
Museum at Harvard University. Putnam was truly enamored of the site
and was the first of many anthropologists to discern the "solar" qualities
of the mound and notice that the setting sun always touched upon the
center of the oval.

Clark and Marjorie Hardman documented the solar alignment of Serpent Mound to the summer solstice in 1987.[15] In the same year, William F. Romain published his archaeoastronomy work regarding lunar alignments based on the curves in the effigy body.

Romain's seminal work in the late 1980s pointed out that there is a true north orientation in archaeoastronomy toward the present pole star, Polaris. Later in the chapter, we will see Romain's argument as to why Scorpius is associated with the archaeoastronomy of the Great Serpent Mound.

In terms of archaeoastronomy or the study of how people in the past "have understood the phenomena in the sky, how they used the phenomena and what role the sky played in their

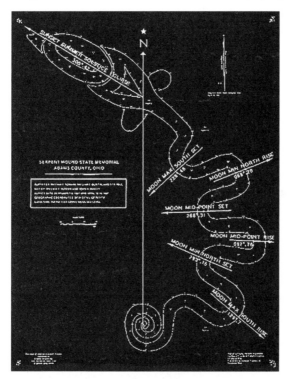

Fig. 8.11. William Romain's diagram detailing the
lunar alignments of the Serpent Mound.
Serpent Mound State Memorial, Adams County, OH, 1987.
Originally published in *Ohio Archaeologist*. Courtesy of William F. Romain

cultures"[16] is abundant across the ancient earthen works, particularly in the Great Serpent Mound. From a cosmological perspective, the image presented of the Great Serpent Mound has roots in many great stories from tribal oral traditions, typically around the serpent chasing and then eating the sun, such as in my Cherokee traditions.

AS ABOVE, SO BELOW:
THE DARK RIFT OF THE MILKY WAY AND
THE JOURNEY OF THE SOULS

Ross Hamilton spends a great deal of his book *Star Mounds: Legacy of a Native American Mystery* presenting the Star Lodge stories of Indigenous peoples in relation to the potential archaeoastronomy of each of the mounds toward specific constellations, although his tribal sources for these assertations are unclear. Painstaking in detail, Hamilton's work culminates with the conclusion of how the Dark Rift of the Milky Way is embodied in a set of related earthen works and tied to the Journey of the Souls.

The reader might recall in the Earth Diver Myth how the stars/souls made their journey here from the distant Pleiades, through the center of the Milky Way, and were then guided by the Morning Star (Venus, our closest planet) to Mother Earth.

The image from Hamilton's work is the representation of the constellations that make up the Dark Rift of the Milky Way aligning to a specific set of earthen works.

It is my hope to verify the methodologies employed by Ross Hamilton and validate the sources of his Star Lodge stories with tribal elders and tribal experts on these stories. And if his alignments of the constellations to the mounds are accurate as well, I would love to plot out the physical map of the below constellations on a map of the greater Ohio River Valley.

Fig. 8.12. Here we see the Dark Rift of the Milky Way superimposed over a template of the Mississippian Earthworks, representing a physical Journey of the Souls, to mirror the Upper Realm. As above, so below.
From *Star Mounds: A Legacy of a Native American Mystery* by Ross Hamilton.
North Atlantic Books, 2012. Courtesy of Ross Hamilton.

AXIS MUNDI: CAHOKIA

Concurrent with this notion is the theory that several earthen work/ natural landscapes were associated with axis mundi sites. Axis mundi, or "center of the world" from an Indigenous cosmological perspective, may take the form of the Tree of Life, a navel of the world, ritual objects, or, sometimes, places. The axis mundi is often centered to the four cardinal directions.

To continue with the example of the Tree of Life as axis mundi, in its branches is the Upper Realm, where reside the Thunder Beings and their messengers the Thunderbirds. Below the horizontal, where the roots of the Tree of Life are, is the Lower Realm, where the Underwater Panther / Serpent leads the Water Spirits.

There are several prominent places of sacred geography that are good examples of a vertical axis mundi: Mount Kunlun for Taoists, Mount Sumeru for Buddhists, Mount Kailiash for Hindus, the Temple Mount for Muslims, King Solomon's Temple for Jews and Christians, Mount Parnassus for Greeks, and, perhaps, the Great Mound at Cahokia.

Romain effectively argues that the Great Mound at Cahokia was indeed one of these axis mundi points. A place where effectively one could experience a comingling of the Upper Realm and the Lower Realm.[17]

The first graphic below explains that the physical geography of the Cahokian complex is surrounded by swampy terrain, but that the complex itself is dry. The takeaway is that the dry area is symbolic of this realm, the earthly realm (that was created when the Upper and Lower Realms intersected and Grandmother Spider wove this Middle Realm) but that the watery / swampy terrain encompassing the complex indicates that it is associated with the Lower Realm, the Underwater Realm.[18]

Next, Romain utilizes lidar imaging (light detection and ranging: a technology that uses lasers and GPS to detect objects beneath vegetation and digitally map landscapes and structures) of the main plazas surrounding the Great Mound at Cahokia to illustrate geometrical associations, in this case, squares. We can see from figure 8.14 that Monk's Mound or Great Mound is at the center of four design squares or groupings of mounds in separate plazas.

Again, we see the axis mundi with the general framework of the four cardinal directions surrounding it. Additionally, there was a large wooden structure surrounded by a palisade located on the top of the Great Mound, and it, too, was situated to four cardinal directions. This wooden structure was the largest of the Mississippian building structures and was likely a "spirit house" that could have been a council house, a chief's house, and perhaps a small place for special burials. Just south of this temple an excavation revealed that there was a very large posthole (11 feet deep and 3 feet in diameter).

Shortly after the excavation, the team placed a smaller diameter yet taller pole (36 feet) wooden post in the hole. Three days later it was struck by lightning. The area is prone to lightning strikes and thunderstorms. A warning sign presently stands as a beacon to beware of lighting and storms. Romain theorizes that this lightning, a spectacular sight indeed, could be a physical symbol of a connection between the Upper and Lower Realms—the lightning, energy from the Upper Realm, strikes the Middle Realm in our world, which is the axis mundi to the watery Lower Realm, and so we have a direct connection to the Journey of the Souls.

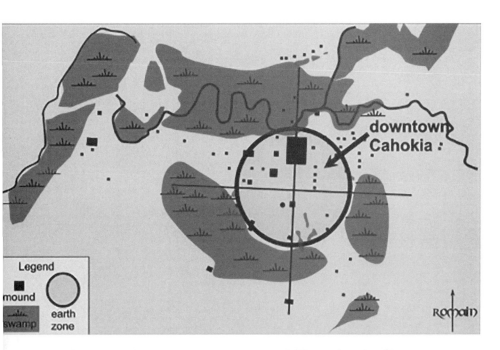

Fig. 8.13. Cahokian axis mundi. Romain's illustration detailing
Monk's Mound as the axis mundi for the Cahokian Mound Complex
as well as comparing the "earth zone" or Middle Realm to the
surrounding watery Lower Realm.
"Monks Mound as an Axis Mundi for the Cahokian World," by William F. Romain, 2017.
Illinois Archaeological Survey, Inc., *Illinois Archaeology*, vol. 29, pp. 27–52.
Used by permission of the Illinois Archaeological Survey.

Fig. 8.14. A digital overlay of the Great Mound at Cahokia, representing an axis mundi among the other earthen works. "Monks Mound as an Axis Mundi for the Cahokian World," by William F. Romain, 2017. Illinois Archaeological Survey, Inc., *Illinois Archaeology*, vol. 29, pp. 27–52. Used by permission of the Illinois Archaeological Survey.

Fig. 8.15. Herb Roe's illustration of a lightning strike on the Cyprus axis mundi atop the grand mound in the grand plaza at Cahokia. A lightning strike would cement the connection between the Upper Realm and the Middle or Earthly Realm in a magical moment.

Digital illustration, all rights held by the artist Herb Roe © 2018

With the related axis mundi in the Newark Complex, through the Hopewell Road, leading to the Mound City Group, we now have two major sites that would enable the devout to ensure that their deceased could, with the forces of nature, or the sun, moon, and sky, help deliver their souls through the Journey of the Souls back home to the stars.

Additional evidence that the Great Mound at Cahokia is an axis mundi is its relationship to the adjoining Woodhenge III, where the equinoctial sun rises over the Great Mound.

Like the measurement unit HMU (1,054 feet), the measurement found in replication at Cahokia was found at the Toltec site. It was 47.5 meters, and multiples of that number.[19] Romain has found that "design squares" were based upon multiples of the Toltec "module," and the largest of the design squares was just south of the primary axis mundi with the Great Mound as the center and the surrounding design squares oriented to the four cardinal directions.

This largest of the design squares encompassed a series of other important architectural elements: Mound 72, Mound 66, and the bisecting vertical "Rattlesnake Causeway" (see fig. 8.16 below). Curiously, the Mound 72 Sub1 Mound held burial remains—the curious "beaded couple" with a young male buried on top of a young female. By the barrage of beads afforded this burial, the couple must have been important. Symbolic of First Man and Mother Corn? The two elaborately clad twin burials in Mound 72 at Cahokia were one man and one female. Perhaps the union of the sacred and the feminine is the true sacred?

In summary, we notice that in figure 8.15 above, the whole Cahokian complex is slightly oriented away from the four cardinal directions' orientation. Specifically, the whole complex is oriented slightly off from true north by five degrees, and that skewing is deliberate on behalf of the builders, because viewed through the lens of Western geometry, we can observe that there are several root 2 rectangles incorporated into the design of Cahokia.

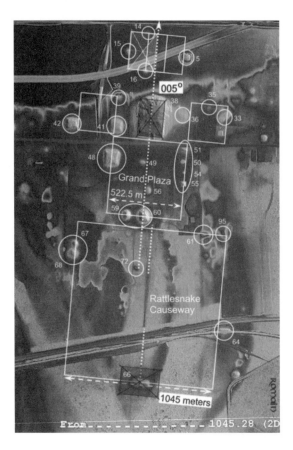

Fig. 8.16. Mathematical interpretations of the Great Mound and surrounding earthen works at Cahokia imply a carefully designed central axis mundi into the complex.

"Monks Mound as an Axis Mundi for the Cahokian World," by William F. Romain, 2017. Illinois Archaeological Survey, Inc., *Illinois Archaeology*, vol. 29, pp. 27–52. Used by permission of the Illinois Archaeological Survey.

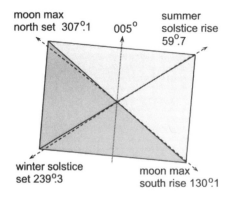

Fig. 8.17. Romain illustrates graphically the reason for the five-degree solar orientation at Monk's Mound at Cahokia.

"Monks Mound as an Axis Mundi for the Cahokian World," by William F. Romain, 2017. Illinois Archaeological Survey, Inc., *Illinois Archaeology*, vol. 29, pp. 27–52. Used by permission of the Illinois Archaeological Survey.

ROOT 2 RECTANGLES

A root 2 rectangle design can be found in the central Great Mound, the North Plaza (two side to side), and south of the Great Mound, thus further illustrating the axis mundi of the overall complex!

As we can see from figure 8.17, the slight tilt five degrees off true north to the east allows the Great Mound and other design rectangles to be oriented to both the sun (summer solstice sunrise and winter solstice set) and the moon (moon max north set and moon max south rise), as well as set the site axis for all of Cahokia to be coincident with the Milky Way Azimuth. It is all connected. From a ceremonial perspective, this could have allowed the participants to witness both the sacred masculine and the sacred feminine, if not simply a symbolic orientation when everything is connected.

THE NEWARK EARTHEN WORKS

Now let us progress further in our understanding of the complexities of the earthen works by examining the masterpiece, the Newark Earthen Works, which cover more than four square miles of a river valley nestled between Racoon Creek and the North and South Forks of the Licking River.

In figure 8.18 we have the 1860 Wyrick Map of the Newark Earthen Works, the pinnacle of the mound builders of the Adena and the Hopewell phases. Below we see an illustration of two simple shapes from this work in the upper left portions of the earthen work. Note the round Observation Circle adjoining the Octagon.

Astronomer John Eddy first discovered the alignment of the earthen works' axis to the moon's maximum north rise in 1978. Subsequently, Ray Hively and Robert Horn discovered the rest of the lunar cycles of the Newark Earthen Works in 1982.[20] Below is an illustration of the findings of Hively and Horn in their archaeoastronomy study that

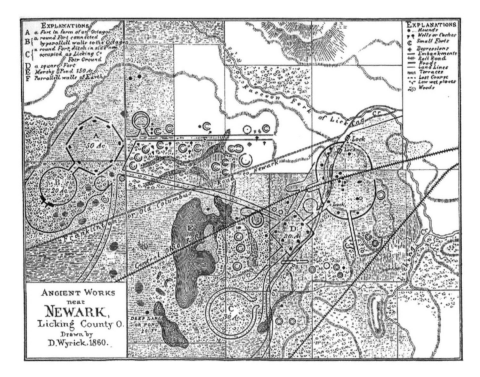

Fig. 8.18. Wyrick Map of the Newark Earthen Works, 1860, providing a glimpse of its ancient glory. Note the Great Circle, one of eight sites in the Hopewell Ceremonial Earthworks designated a UNESCO World Heritage Site in 2023.
Wikimedia Commons

proved that the two works are aligned so as to chronicle the movements of the moon to its minimum and maximum moonrise and moonset in the north and the south every 18.61 years, due to the slow precession of the moon's orbit.

The Newark Earthen Works, in the words of Squier and Davis in their chapter "Sacred Enclosures," are described as "so complicated, that it is impossible to give anything like a comprehensible description of them."

The Newark Earthen Works are complicated, but as we take one perspective at a time, it is easier to digest it. The example below shows the basics of archaeoastronomy and the alignment of the earthen works to movements of the moon and the sun.

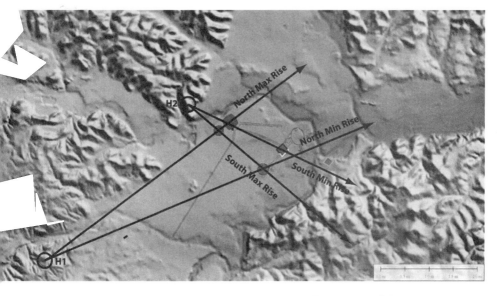

Fig. 8.19a. A 1982 illustration of the lunar alignments of the
Newark Earthen Works by Ray Hively and Robert Horn.

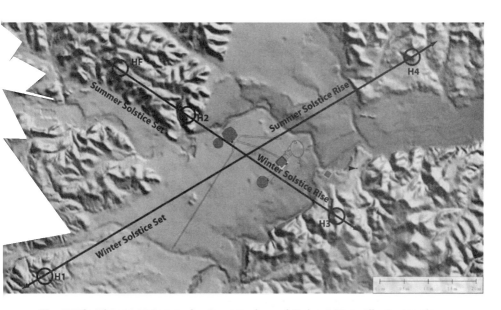

Fig. 8.19b. This 1982 image by Ray Hively and Robert Horn illustrates the
archaeoastronomy of the solstices at the Newark Earthen Works.

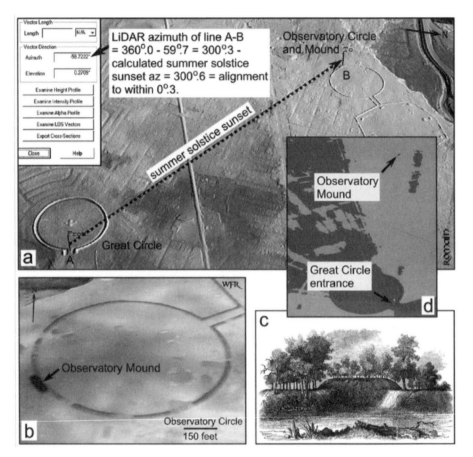

Fig. 8.20. This digital overlay of the solstice alignments is superimposed over a lidar map of the Newark Earthen Works and of the Great Circle and an observatory mound.

"Adena-Hopewell Earthworks and the Milky Way Path of Souls," by William F. Romain. In *Tracing the Relational: The Archaeology of Worlds, Spirits, and Temporalities.* University of Utah Press, Salt Lake City, 2015. Reprinted courtesy of the University of Utah Press.

In another section of the Newark Earthen Works, the Great Circle and the "Thunderbird Mound" are oriented to the minimum moonrise in the north at 67.5 degrees. Also, there is a summer solstice sunset observation orientation from the entrance of the Great Circle over the Observatory Circle. Beyond the Octagon and the Observatory Circle, we have the Great Circle, Wright Square, the Ellipse, Salisbury Square, Geller Hill, and ultimately, the Great

Hopewell Road (see the 1862 annotated Salisbury Map, courtesy of the American Antiquarian Society).[21]

While a natural part of the landscape, Geller Hill is located a mile southwest of the Observatory Circle and Octagon earthen work and is in the line of sight of the Newark Earthen Works complex, and an important component of the works, as we shall explore.

An example is shown in Romain's illustration of various alignments, such as the triangular alignment of the Great Circle, the Observatory Circle, and Geller Mound with the summer solstice sunset (see fig. 8.21 below) at the Newark Earthen Works. By connecting these three sights, we end up with an isosceles triangle, with the two earthen works having the exact same angle, with the corresponding sides equaling 7 HMU or 7,378 feet. Incidentally, 1 Hopewell Measurement Unit is also equal to the diameter of the Observatory Circle (so 1 HMU was used to design the observatory circle). Also, with the Octagon, each of the sides is one

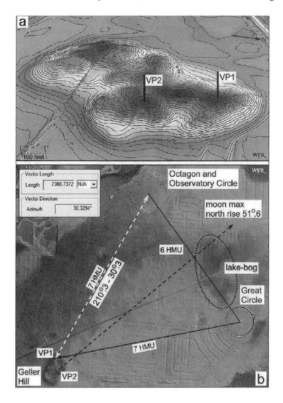

Fig. 8.21. This linear map of the Newark Earthen Works mathematically illustrates the triangular alignment of the Great Circle, the Observatory Circle, and Geller Mound is oriented to the moon's maximum moonrise. "Adena-Hopewell Earthworks and the Milky Way Path of Souls," by William F. Romain. In *Tracing the Relational: The Archaeology of Worlds, Spirits, and Temporalities*. University of Utah Press, Salt Lake City, 2015. Reprinted courtesy of the University of Utah Press.

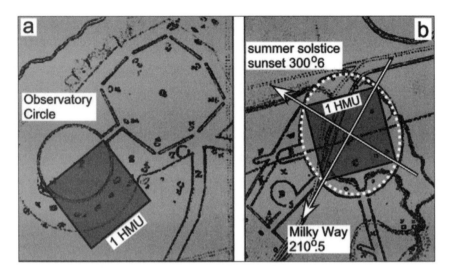

Fig. 8.22. This drawing illustrates the Great Octagon and Circle alignments to the summer solstice and the ground trajectory of the Milky Way.
Courtesy of the American Antiquarian Society and William F. Romain

HMU. From the vantage point of Geller Hill, on the night of the moon's maximum moonrise, an observer would see the moon rise precisely between the two adjoining works.[22]

In the same vein as the Observatory Circle and the Octagon, the Ellipse at Newark also seems to incorporate archaeoastronomy elements. Romain has noted that at the cluster of 17 mounds above Wright's Square, if an ellipse were drawn over the cluster, based off a square of 1 HMU, the resulting diagonal axis will point to (1) summer solstice sunset and (2) the ground trajectory of the Milky Way on the night of the summer solstice, following the sunset. Recall that this is the second of the summer solstice observation points within the same complex.[23]

From here, we advance to the Great Hopewell Road. The Hopewell Road is not a typical road, as Romain deduces with cross-sectioned lidar that the Great Hopewell Road was a concave pathway with walls built up on either side. There are similar concave pathways with walls at the Portsmouth, Mariette, High Bank, Hopeton, and Fort Ancient sites. In each of these cases these "parallel walls" are all lined up with solstice azimuths.

Amazingly, on the summer solstice during the era of Hopewell, when the Milky Way is at its brightest, the Hopewell Road and the trajectory of the Milky Way mirrored each other, extending from the northeast at an azimuth of about 30 degrees, heading across the sky, to finally plunge in the southwest at an azimuth of about 210 degrees.

To complicate the rarity of these events transpiring, the trajectories of the sun, moon, and stars all had to line up. First, once every nine and one-half years either the Octagon or the Great Circle came into alignment with the moon's maximum north or minimum north limit. Next, the "date of the summer solstice narrowed the target time down to the month and day within the designated lunar year. Nightfall was the final tick of the clock" and at sunset, the sky above the Hopewell Road at one end filled with the Dark Rift of the Milky Way, and by the time it passed overhead, one could walk along with it above one's head, and by the time you finished on the walking journey, it had descended out of the sky over the horizon and out of sight.[24]

What does all this mean? To answer that question, we need to review the cosmology defined elsewhere in this work. Specifically, we will remember the Upper Realm and the Lower Realm, with the Tree of Life as the axis mundi, the Upper Realm as the sky realm, and the Lower Realm often as the watery world of the Underwater Serpent / Panther. And recall that the Journey of the Souls is the soul's astrogenesis journey from the Seven Sisters constellation of Pleiades, along the Dark Rift of the Milky Way, guided by the Morning Star / Venus (the closest planet to Earth) to our home here on Earth. And then when our journey is complete, we return on the same path.

Thus, the keepers of the Newark Earthen Works would chronicle the movements of the stars until they knew the exact year, month, day, and time when all the celestial bodies lined up in a way that allowed the Upper Realm to mirror itself on the landscape of the Earth Mother, and thus allow us to live the precept "as above, so below." But the significance of the Dark Rift of the Milky Way in the Journey of the Souls is important, the one act of the faithful: "As in heaven on Earth."[25]

As beautiful as this act is, there is more archaeoastronomy to the Newark complex. Referring to figure 8.23, we see that Romain has suggested that several of the causeways and causeway sections could have been "orientated along celestial azimuths." The Section 1 causeway was "apparently orientated to within one degree of a due east-west line," which is either the Line of the Sun (where it rises and sets) and/or the direction of the equinox rise and set.

Causeway Section 2, facing to the northeast of Wright's Square, was oriented to the moon's north minimum set, before it arcs toward the Octagon. And as mentioned before, the major axis of the Great Circle, via the Thunderbird Mound, is oriented to the moon's minimum north rise, which turns into another walled walkway.

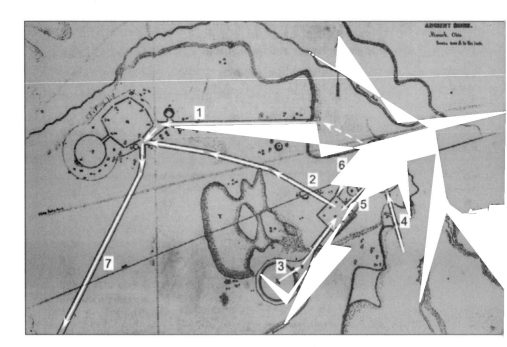

Fig. 8.23. This map details the individual locations of important sacred spots and causeways in the Newark Earthen Works.
Courtesy of the American Antiquarian Society and William F. Romain

The Observatory Circle, Causeway Section 3, which, as stated before, was oriented to the moon's minimum northern rise, is also adjacent to the Octagon and therefore the gateway (Causeway Section 7) to the walled walkway, the Great Hopewell Road, which we determined was oriented to the ascension and descension of the Dark Rift of the Milky Way, otherwise known as the Journey of the Souls, the place of Indigenous origin. Causeway Section 7 points to the summer solstice sunset and the ground trajectory of the Milky Way on the summer solstice, following the sunset. Near Causeway Sections 5 and 6 is potentially an observation point for onlookers to the main event, those souls or people accompanying them on their final leg of the Journey of the Souls.

ALL ROADS LEAD TO SACRED GEOGRAPHY

If one follows the trajectory from the Causeway Section 7 to the Great Hopewell Road, you find it eventually runs into the Mound City Group, a unique Hopewell earthen works complex. Romain has demonstrated that both the Great Hopewell Road and the Mound City Group are both aligned to the Milky Way.

There are no fewer than five additional sites aligned with nearby Sugarloaf Mountain (see fig. 8.24b). A visitor to Stitt Mound would see the winter solstice sunrise over Sugarloaf as would a visitor to either Mound City or Adena Mound, and they could view the moon's minimum north rise over Sugarloaf. From the small circle at the Hopeton Earthen Works to the Shriver Circle, one could witness the summer solstice sunrise over Sugarloaf.

From the vantage point of Sugarloaf, four earthen works are aligned to the cardinal directions: Circleville 14 miles to the north, Marietta 79 miles to the east, Portsmouth 46 miles to the south, and Fort Ancient 62 miles to the west.[26] Remember the cosmological Tree of Life as an axis mundi and the four corners holding up the sky and this orientation of these other earthen works to the four directions, and we find a much deeper meaning to this design.

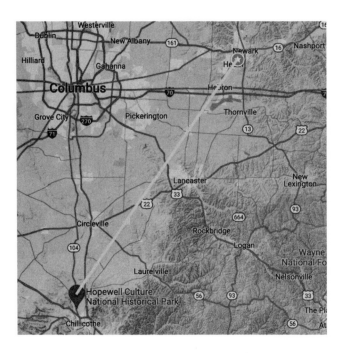

Fig. 8.24a. Map illustrating the latest LiDAR (Light Detection and Ranging) rediscovering of the ceremonial path of the Great Hopewell Road of the Newark Earthen Works complex leading to the Mound City Group. Previously it was thought to lead to the Axis Mundi of Sugarloaf Mountain.
Map data ©2024 Google

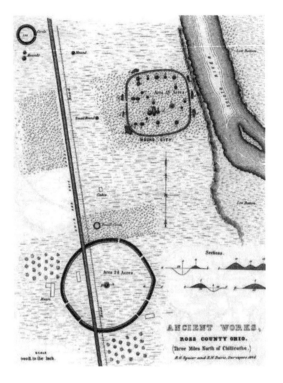

Fig. 8.24b. This illustrative map from Squier and Davis, c. 1848, details the 25 mound group and how it looked over 150 years ago.
Wikimedia Commons

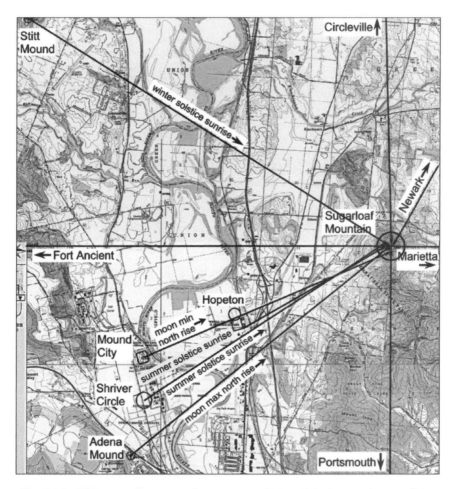

Fig. 8.24c. This map illustrates that Sugarloaf Mountain is an axis mundi to surrounding mound complexes, including solar and lunar alignments.
"Adena-Hopewell Earthworks and the Milky Way Path of Souls," by William F. Romain. In *Tracing the Relational: The Archaeology of Worlds, Spirits, and Temporalities*. University of Utah Press, Salt Lake City, 2015. Reprinted courtesy of the University of Utah Press.

THE JOURNEY OF THE SOULS AND THE DARK RIFT OF THE MILKY WAY

As previously discussed, the Hopewell Road of the Newark Complex is oriented for a viewer to clearly see the Dark Rift of the Milky Way when the sun, moon, and stars are properly aligned. We also recall that the Hopewell Road points to Mound City. Romain argues convincingly that this over 100-mile network of complexes allows for what would be a massive ceremonial complex. Based off the cosmological Creation Story (the Earth Diver Myth, specifically the Dhegiha version "In the Beginning our Souls were like Stars in the Sky"), we correlate that this ceremonial complex is strongly associated with that cosmological story. Within this complex, ceremonial participants could view and mark important movements of the moon and view the sunrise and sunsets on the summer and winter solstices, and some could also walk along the Hopewell Road at sunset (when all the conditions were aligned) with the Dark Rift of the Milky Way visible above their heads as they made the pilgrimage to Mound City, which is also oriented to the same stellar alignment.

I posit that this was part of a ceremonial rite of passage that perhaps occurred over the course of the four seasons of the year, culminating in the final portion of the ceremony occurring on the summer solstice and through the night (see "The Ceremonies of Ceremonies" on page 158).

SCORPIUS AND THE GREAT SERPENT CATCHES THE SUN

Recalling the Dhegiha version of the Earth Diver myth, the Journey of the Souls begins and ends with the Seven Sisters constellation, or Pleiades, and it occurs across the Dark Rift of the Milky Way and finds Earth via the Morning Star.

In many tribal traditions, there is a keeper at the gate who does or doesn't allow a soul to pass and to return home. In some cases, there is an old woman / old man gatekeeper there and sometimes a Great Serpent gatekeeper to the Realm of the Dead, as identified by many of the Algonquian-speaking tribes. Remember that the Great Serpent is also known as the Underwater Panther / Serpent to a broad number of Algonquian- and Siouan-speaking tribes. But the Underwater Panther / Serpent also has wings and can be seen in the Middle and the Upper Realms, and in some cases, can be seen in the summer months flying in the sky.[27]

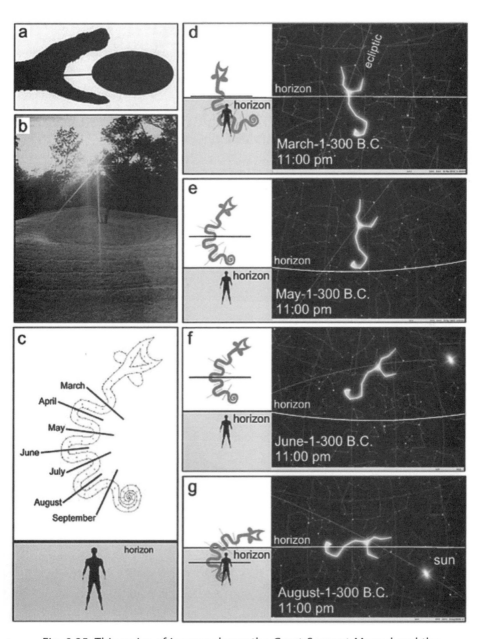

Fig. 8.25. This series of images shows the Great Serpent Mound and the
ensuing solar alignments in 1 to 300 BCE with Scorpius, illustrating the
"serpent eating the sun" of tribal lore.

"Adena-Hopewell Earthworks and the Milky Way Path of Souls," by William F. Romain. In
Tracing the Relational: The Archaeology of Worlds, Spirits, and Temporalities. University of
Utah Press, Salt Lake City, 2015. Reprinted courtesy of the University of Utah Press.

Thus, we find a connection between the Great Serpent Mound, the Great Serpent as the gatekeeper of the Realm of the Dead, and all three within the constellation of Scorpius. Besides being connected through the Indigenous oral traditions of the eastern Woodlands customs, Romain offers an enticing theory related to the stars. The constellation of Scorpius and its neighbor star Antares offer a stellar version of the Great Serpent. See figure 8.25 on page 157.

The Great Serpent Mound is also in geographic proximity to Sugarloaf Mountain (see fig. 8.24), which ties all these great earthen works to the axis mundi of Sugarloaf for the Journey of the Souls. We recall the layout of the Great Serpent Mound, with the Great Serpent poised to bite the "oval."

And now we come to Romain's new informed interpretations. The archaeoastronomy of the Great Serpent Mound, when viewed with Scorpius in mind, becomes poetic. A thousand-plus years ago in the spring, Scorpius rises out of the Southern Hemisphere or Lower Realm and moves up into the Northern Hemisphere or Upper Realm, traveling along the ecliptic (annual path of the sun) and slowly rotating clockwise, until by the end of the summer, Scorpius crosses over to the Lower Realm once again, but this time almost catching the sun. Today, many tribes still recount this act in our great stories of the Serpent attacking the sun.

THE CEREMONY OF CEREMONIES

The two initiates have been in teachings for the better part of four years. They have been coming every season, governed by the cycles of the moon, sun, and stars. The two initiates have seen the Grand Ceremony once, years before, but only from afar and from one of the visitation mounds that was designed for visitors. Now they stand at the beginning of the Great Road, after having watched the sun rise and set from different vantage points in the Great Circle and the Great Octagon.

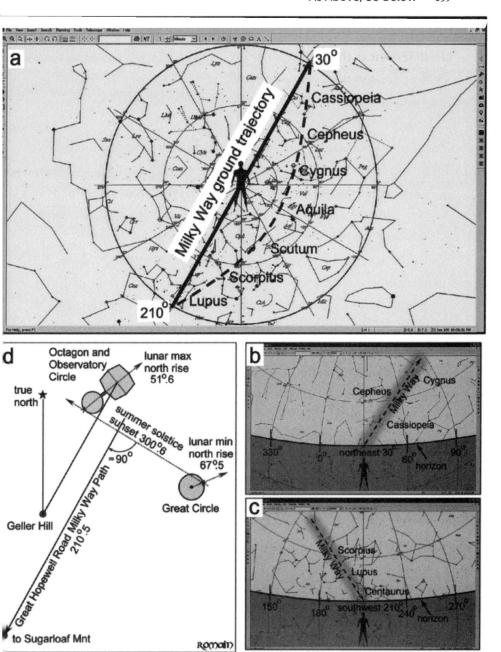

Fig. 8.26. This set of stellar maps illustrates how the Great Hopewell Road
aligns with the Dark Rift of the Milky Way, or the Journey of the Souls.
"Adena-Hopewell Earthworks and the Milky Way Path of Souls," by William F. Romain. In
Tracing the Relational: The Archaeology of Worlds, Spirits, and Temporalities. University of
Utah Press, Salt Lake City, 2015. Reprinted courtesy of the University of Utah Press.

The two initiates have been through many ceremonies like this, but not to the same degree as the Ceremony of Ceremonies. For years they have trained and prepared. Only once every nine years would the stars, sun, and moon line up for this grand nighttime ceremony.

The teachings were the secrets of the Order, and the only way to truly understand the mound complex that lay before them was to pledge the Order and endure the trials of each teaching and attain the next rank within the Order. There were many teachings, all translated into their own dialect of their Indigenous language.

Sometimes the teachings were stories, which could last for days if not even weeks. Some of the stories were so old that they spoke of the time when most of the northern lands were frozen over and covered in ice. Some of the stories went back to the time before the beginning of time here on Turtle Island. Those stories went back before the crossing across the galaxy from the real homelands, nestled in the Seven Sisters constellation.

Many of the teachings were songs, and like the stories, some of the songs could last all night or sometimes for days and weeks. There were honoring songs for everything: from the people themselves to the Earth Mother, the Waters, the Fish, the Plant Nations, Food Plants, Medicine Herbs, the Animal Nations, the Trees, the Birds, the Four Winds, the Thunder Beings, the Sun, Grandmother Moon, the Stars, and the Sacred Mountain that sits waiting for them in this ceremony, for the Teachers who taught us all of these sacred teachings, how to remember who we really are and where we come from, and how to make it back home, the real home, on the Journey of the Souls, back to the Seven Sisters. And finally, there were the songs for the Creator, who brought them all here from across the stars.

Many of the teachings were of healing and humility. Some of the lessons were hard lessons to learn: how to make oneself devoid of ego and pain, how to embrace the smallness of oneself versus the incredible beauty and magnitude of the wonderful power of life that inhabited all of Mother Earth that was all sacred and a gift to us from Creator and Spirit. There were teachings to remind us that we are to respect the Covenants between us and the Plant Nations, between us and the Animal Councils.

TEN THOUSAND YEARS AGO AND BEYOND

The Antiquity of Indigenous Peoples in America

William F. Romain's epic work *An Archaeology of the Sacred: Adena-Hopewell Astronomy and Landscape Archaeology* serves as such an inspiration for me as a Native soul who was more than curious about the ancient earthen works but wanted more than the original (1848) Squier and Davis *Ancient Monuments of the Mississippi Valley* had to offer.

While working on this project, a few books lie close to my desk and are all dog-eared and much loved. Tim Pauketat's *Cahokia*, Robert L. Hall's *An Archaeology of the Soul*, and the anthology around *Picture Cave* are mainstays. I have studied nearly everything that William F. Romain has published or printed.

But an article published by Romain in 2011 crept into my world, and it is where I choose to begin with the story of the ancient earthen works.

Historically, the oldest Mounds were thought to be at Poverty Point, Louisiana, and its carbon dating yielded a date of around 1500–1700 BCE / 3500–3700 BP! Poverty Point is one of the most fascinating of the ancient earthen works. The complex at Poverty Point covers over 400 acres and includes the second largest mound north of Mesoamerica.

Lidar utilizes reflected near-infrared laser beams aimed at the earth

Fig. 9.1. This map of North America pinpoints the
location of the Poverty Point site.
"Astronomy and Geometry at Poverty Point," by William F. Romain and Norman L. Davis.
Louisiana Archaeology, no. 38. Courtesy of William F. Romain.

from an aircraft to develop images devoid of the overgrowth of flora and fauna. Lidar has helped the archaeological field better understand the intricate design of the Poverty Point complex.

Lidar results from 2013 help us visualize the complex as "a series of concentric C-shaped ridges" composed of five to six mounds, six concentric ridges with swales in between and crosscut by two to three aisles, a central plaza, and borrow pits.

Temporal sequencing of the total Poverty Point Mound complex suggests construction took place between 1600 BCE and 1300 BCE and that a case should be made that the complexity of the design must have been coordinated if not fully designed to "transform the landscape into a preconceived and desired form" based upon the "site orientation, celestial alignments, bilateral symmetry of design points, internal geometry . . . and local topography."[1]

The largest earthen works, Mound A, is both a combination mound and a conical mound with a ramp. The length of the work is just under

700 feet and it is thought to have been built fairly rapidly, in a span of months.

Mound C is an oval-shaped conical, which immediately suggests that this site has a north-south orientation to its design, perhaps for viewing. The construction of Mound C is unique, as its base structure is composed of sixteen different thin layers of various colors and textures. The final singular, conical layer was all one material. The various materials include hematite, red ochre, and crystalline quartz, all of which are still used ceremonially to this day. This feels to me like its construction was indeed ceremonial and full of meaning, if not "sacred and ceremonial."

Most interesting about Mound C is that it served as an observation mound, as it was oriented so that the viewer could witness and experience the solstices. Mound C was also situated on the major north-south axis of

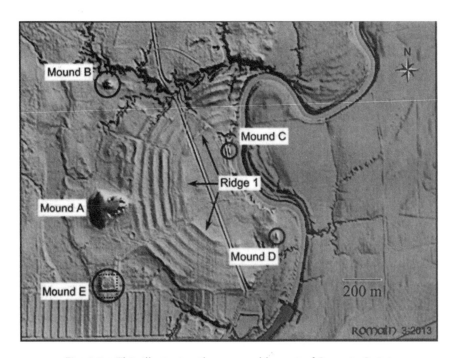

Fig. 9.2a. This illustrates the general layout of Poverty Point
with major mounds detailed.
"Astronomy and Geometry at Poverty Point," by William F. Romain and Norman L. Davis.
Louisiana Archaeology, no. 38. Courtesy of William F. Romain.

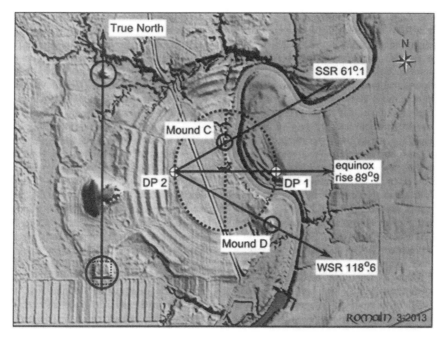

Fig. 9.2b. A lidar image showing sunrise alignments.
SSR = summer solstice rise; WSR = winter solstice rise.
"Astronomy and Geometry at Poverty Point," by William F. Romain and Norman L. Davis.
Louisiana Archaeology, no. 38. Courtesy of William F. Romain.

the inner oval, giving further symmetry to the overall design. Additionally, viewed from Mound C, the winter solstice sun will appear to set into the side of Mound A.

One of the more interesting mathematical design elements of the complex incorporates a notion known as a solstice triangle, illustrated below. A solstice triangle is an equilateral triangle that, when one of the sides is oriented to true north, the other two sides of the triangle are congruent with the solstice azimuths. This will be more clearly interpreted and illustrated later in this chapter when we discuss solstice triangles in greater detail regarding Watson Brake.

There are also elements of asymmetrical design incorporated into the complex regarding the solstices. Examine the ellipse illustrated in (figs. 9.2b and c). From the two illustrations, we see that the ellipse is oriented to the celestial north pole by connecting Mound D to

Mound C. A true east-west design line connects Design Point 1 (DP1) to Design Point 2 (DP2), ensuring that the four cardinal directions are a central part of this ceremonial complex.

Design Point 1 is an interesting but necessary component to the complex, as it gives an eastern counterbalance to the western-oriented Design Point 2 (DP2). The line connecting them is often referred to as "the line of the sun," meaning it rises in the east and sets in the west, an important ceremonial marker to many tribes to this day.

Water is also an important design element in the eastern part of the ellipse complex. The great "old one" or the Mississippi lies in proximity at 15.5 miles away and is situated in the Bayou Marcon, which sprawls across the Mississippi Delta. Design Point 1 (DP1) lies in the watery areas of the bayou, and some have conjectured that it might have been under water at

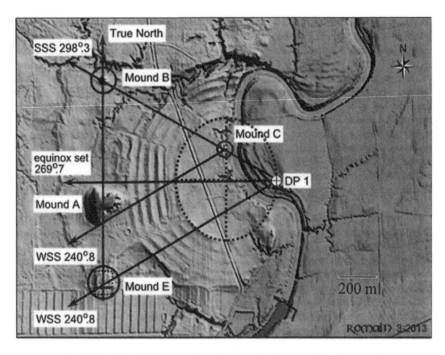

Fig. 9.2c. A lidar image showing posited sunset alignments.
SSS = summer solstice set; WSS = winter solstice set.
"Astronomy and Geometry at Poverty Point," by William F. Romain and Norman L. Davis.
Louisiana Archaeology, no. 38. Courtesy of William F. Romain.

some point in the past. Regardless of whether it was under water or not, it was an important design element for the site and brings balance and harmony at an axis mundi site where the Upper and Lower Realms meet.

The role of water in these ceremonial complexes often has connotations of the Lower Realm, associated with the Earth Mother, fertility, and the Underwater Panther and, overall, the sacred feminine.

The role of solstice sunrises and sunsets are important as well. Viewed from DP2, the summer solstice sun will rise over Mound C, the winter solstice sunrise over Mound D, and the equinox sunrise over DP1 from this vantage point. Conversely, DP1 viewers could witness the summer and winter solstice sunsets, as well as the equinox sunset.

To summarize and hypothesize what may have been going on at this site and time. Romain and his team used celestial techniques with Starry Night Pro to align the site with historical and sacred movements of the sun, the moon, and the four directions.

There is clearly a well-planned overall design, which is mind-boggling considering it was built over 3,700 years before present (BP). The site was intentionally oriented toward celestial north. This is easily seen in the representations of the ellipse, whose central axis lies perfectly north-south at the 1700 BCE period. Mound C is also perfectly aligned on the same north-south axis.

I concur with Romain who believes that Mound C was the most ideal location from which to observe the solstices, and its unique construction using different layers (stratigraphy) points to a careful homage to the soil and other earthen representations of Mother Earth. The fact that artifacts such as hematite, crystalline quartz, and, especially, red ochre have been found suggests that this was a sacred ceremonial spot and whatever rites were practiced here were aligned to the seasons and the rhythms of the mother.

There is a duality to the entire design. Notice the Design Points 1 and 2 in relation to the ellipse. From one vantage point, ceremonial participants could witness winter and summer solstice sunrises; from the other design point, they could witness winter and summer solstice sunsets.

Remember that a true celestial north has strong overtones of the axis mundi, with the earth literally seemingly to be the center of the universe as it spins around us. The entire complex was oriented to the celestial north, thus making the entire site an axis mundus, and therefore probably tied to the ceremony of the Journey of the Souls, over 2500 years before the Mississippian era. This must be the beginning of it all. No, not even close.

WATSON BRAKE MOUND

Situated in the floodplain of the Ouachita River near the present-day city of Monroe in northern Louisiana, Watson Brake is (so far) the oldest celestially aligned mound complex in North America.[2] Consisting of at least eleven mounds ranging from 3 feet to 25 feet tall, they are connected by earthen ridge elements forming an ellipse-shaped oval.

Extensive coring and stratigraphic studies, in addition to twenty-five radiocarbon dates and six luminescence dates, yielded that construction began at this "middle archaic" site around 3500 BCE / 5,500 BP and that most of the construction was completed within a five-hundred-year time frame, thus ending around 3000 BCE. This date of 3500 BCE is nearly two thousand years before Poverty Point. It is the same time frame as ancient Mesopotamia, five hundred years before the rise of the Egyptian civilization where most of the world are hunter-gatherers, and the use of the wheel is spreading out from Mesopotamia. Archaeological remains were detected in the construction of the mound complex, included fire-cracked rocks and fired clay and loam objects, which lends weight toward it having a ceremonial basis.[3]

Figure 9.4 from Romain's lidar work gives us a basic understanding of the layout of the celestially aligned mound complex. Note the ellipse shape and the tilted orientation toward north.

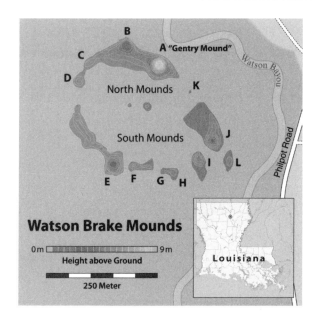

Fig. 9.3. Dorrbecker's map of Watson Brake Mounds in northern Louisiana.
Wikimedia Commons

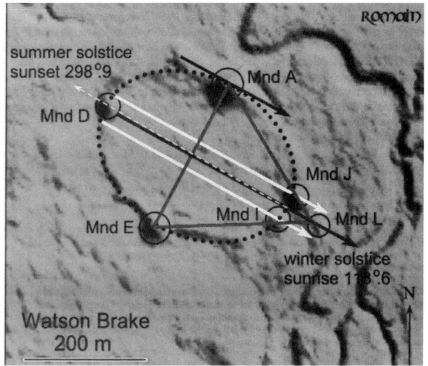

Fig. 9.4. The general layout of the celestially aligned mound complex.
"Editor's Introduction: Email from William Romain." *Louisiana Archaeology*, no. 36, 2009.
Courtesy of William F. Romain.

This ellipse incorporates the previously mentioned Solstice Triangle, where, when one of the sides of an equilateral triangle is aligned to the north, the two remaining sides will correspond in alignment to the solstice azimuths of winter summer sunrise and summer solstice sunset, although in this earliest version, compared to Poverty Point, the longer axis of the ellipse is east to west rather than north to south.

Regardless of the small variations, the site was oriented to a viewer, probably a ceremonial participant, so one could watch the sunrise on the shortest day of the year and sunset on the longest day of the year. Within the context of antiquity, this is an amazing landmark of achievement for Indigenous peoples, illustrating a great understanding of the sun, moon, and stars to the point of mastering the sciences of measuring time and space together in a poetic union.

ANCIENT FLORIDIAN SHELL
AND MIDDEN MOUNDS

Today we refer to the ancient homelands of the Seminole and Miccosukee as Florida, and these lands are lush and rich with biodiverse life and food for ancient hunting and gathering tribal peoples. Human interactions with the land can be connected back to at least twelve thousand years ago. Many of these interactions between humans and the land helped to transform the very geography of the region, gradually over thousands of years. This transformation of the landscape began by the depositing of shells as early as 7,500 years ago when formal centers for dwelling were constructed throughout the coastal and interior zones during much of the Middle and Late Holocene.[4]

The question is raised immediately as we ponder the antiquity of the land: Who influenced whom? Did the big bang of Cahokia affect ancient Florida, or was the influence from somewhere else? Archaeological evidence of an abundance of St. John's-style pottery found at Poverty Point from ancient Florida proves trade and social interactions with presumed respectful intentions going back for many thousands of years. And there is evidence for nonlocal objects from the regions surrounding Cahokia and Macon Plateau.

But what about today? What do these historical "place-making" mounds and, in some cases, practically human-constructed islands and landscapes by ancient Indigenous peoples mean in the place we now call Florida?

In 2005, in the wake of Hurricane Wilma, individuals from the National Park Service began to explore the area now known as the Ten Thousand Islands, an intricate set of mangrove-laden islets on Florida's southwestern coast. The 120-mile-an-hour winds had torn off the thin veneer of vegetation, and the NPS staff archaeologist Margo Schwadron remarked with astonishment at what they saw:

"We'd pull up to an island and see this bank of oyster shells rising eight to ten feet out of the water. Then you'd climb up and realize there was so much more." What they found was extremely large, sculpted mounds, ridges, ramps, plazas, basins, and canals that in some places covered over one hundred acres at a stretch. "There were entire islands, whole landscapes, that people had constructed from shell, it was mind boggling." Radiocarbon dating from that site dates back 3500 years before present.[5]

Another fascinating ancient midden mound, aptly titled "Turtle Mound," is south of what is now the southeast coast of Florida. The largest shell midden on the mainland of the United States, it towers at over 50 feet tall with a length of nearly 600 feet alongside the Indian River and is estimated to contain 35,000 cubic yards.[6] National Park Service records indicate the construction of the shell midden mound to be somewhere between 800 CE and 1400 CE, but radiocarbon dating estimates date the construction of Turtle Mound somewhere around 1000 BCE.

Perhaps Turtle Mound itself is influenced by the turtle in the Earth Diver mythology, the reason we call this Indigenous land "Turtle Island." See figure 9.5 on the next page.

Fig. 9.5. Historical photo of Turtle Mound, circa 1915.
Wikimedia Commons

The antiquity of the ancient earthen works is beyond question, and the question of why points toward understanding the landscapes that we find sacred for their relationship to us as human beings and our relationship to the land and to the sun, moon, and stars.

The movement of the sun and the moon affects us all on a profound level, whether it is the light of the day or the waves of the ocean and the waters of life of the sacred feminine. We look to the sky for inspiration and answers to the basic questions of life, such as "Who are we and where do we come from?"

This work has been a journey backward in time for me as I explored my tribal roots and the cosmologies of my ancient ancestors. It is a cultural interpretation perspective of these roots that I hope can serve as a strong foundation for a glimpse of hope for the future of all humanity.

The Earth is our mother, and it is incumbent upon us all to provide a thriving planet and living ecosystem for the future seven generations. What are we doing to ensure the strength of the Plant and Animal

Nations? What are we doing to ensure that we protect the sanctity of the land and the water? How can we better protect the sacred geography of America?

Listen to the song of the cottonwoods. What do you hear in the wind?

NOTES

1. COSMOGENESIS

1. Napolskikh, "The Earth-Diver Myth (A812)," 120–140.
2. Duncan, *Picture Cave: Unraveling the Mysteries of the Mississippian Cosmos,* chap. 17.
3. Diaz-Granados, *Picture Cave.*
4. Red Corn, Kathryn, *Picture Cave,* chap. 13.
5. Duncan, *Picture Cave,* chap. 17.
6. Pauketat, *Cahokia: Ancient America's Great City on the Mississippi.*
7. Dieterle, "The Redhorn Panel of Picture Cave: An American Star Map."

2. AN ISLAND IN THE EAST

1. Teuton, *Cherokee Stories of the Turtle Island Liars Club,* 49–53.
2. Gardner, *The Origin of God,* 87.
3. Wegener, *The Origin of Continents and Oceans.*
4. Spence, *The History of Atlantis.*
5. Spence, 16.
6. Flem-Ath, *The Atlantis Blueprint,* 6.
7. Spence, 17.
8. Spence, 17.
9. Menzies, *Lost Empire of Atlantis,* 7.
10. Menzies, 3–7.
11. Menzies, 46–47.
12. Menzies, 55.
13. Menzies, 60, 75–79.

3. THE FOUNDERS' DILEMMA OF AMERICA

1. Newell, *Brethren by Nature.*
2. Ehler, *Church and State through the Centuries.*
3. Pope Alexander VI, *Inter Caetera.*
4. Dunbar-Ortiz, *Indigenous Peoples' History.*
5. Johnson, 21 U.S. 543.
6. Newell, 8.
7. Newell, 4.
8. Newell, 6.
9. Newell, 4–7.
10. Waldman, *Atlas of the North American Indian,* 206.
11. Wishart, *An Unspeakable Sadness.*
12. Page, *In the Hands of the Great Spirit,* 104–5.
13. Starita, *I Am a Man,* 17.
14. Starita, 19.
15. Worster, *A River Running West,* 111–112.
16. Gosart, Ulia "The Idea of the Vanishing Race. Who's Vanishing? Curtis' Idea on Race and his Work (1/6)."
17. Merk, *Manifest Destiny and Mission in American History,* 3.
18. Hudson, *Mistress of Manifest Destiny.*
19. Worster, 93.
20. Worster, vi.
21. Worster, vii.
22. Worster, 96.
23. Worster, 96.
24. Worster, 388.
25. Worster, 397, 400.
26. Powell, "On Limitations To The Use of Some Anthropological Data."
27. Dillehay et al., "Monte Verde: Seaweed, Food, Medicine," 784–786.
28. Deloria, *God Is Red,* 69.
29. Deloria, 73.
30. Starita, *I Am a Man.*
31. Deloria, 72.
32. Deloria, 81–83.
33. Deloria, 203, 263–265.
34. Deloria, 261.

4. LIVING RED

1. Interview and conversations with Odawa elder and teacher Dr. Cecil King. 2011–2012.
2. Deloria, *God Is Red*, 176–77.
3. Stoecker, William B., "The Dragon Factor: Why Do Some Believe the Myths Could be Truer than We Thought?" *Atlantis Rising*, no. 119 September/October 2016.
4. Stoecker, "The Dragon Factor."
5. Porter, J. R., *The Lost Bible*, chap. 3.

5. PAHUK

1. Personal interview, Cherie Beam-Calloway, 7/29/2016.
2. Nabokov, *Where the Lightning Strikes,* chap. 10.
3. Beam-Calloway interview.
4. Nabokov, chap. 10.
5. Grinnell, *Pawnee Hero Stories and Folk Tales,* 163–164.
6. Grinnell, 164–170.
7. Nabokov, chap. 10; and Parks, "Pawnee Geography," 153.
8. Blasing, "Pawnee Animal Lodges Revisited."
9. Murie, *Ceremonies of the Pawnee,* 266–268; and Parks "Pawnee Geography," 153–154.
10. Parks, "Pawnee Geography," 10–11, 151–152.
11. Chandler, *The Winged: An Upper Missouri River Ethno-ornithology,* 24.
12. Sandoz, *Love Song to the Plains.*

6. MOTHER CORN, MOTHER EARTH

1. Center for the Electronic Reconstruction of Historical and Archaeological Sites, University of Cincinnati.
2. Fletcher, "The Omaha Tribe," 74, 376.
3. Fenton, *The Iroquois Eagle Dance.*
4. Fletcher, "The Omaha Tribe," 74.
5. Fletcher, "The Omaha Tribe," 74–75.
6. Fletcher, "The Omaha Tribe," 380.
7. Fletcher, "The Omaha Tribe," 376–377.
8. Fletcher, "The Omaha Tribe," 379.
9. Hall, *An Archaeology of the Soul,* 49–50.

10. Fenton, *The Iroquois Eagle Dance,* 189.

11. Fletcher, "The Omaha Tribe," 74.

12. Fletcher, Alice, "The Hako; A Pawnee Ceremony," *American Ethnology,* Part 2. Washington, D.C., 1904.

13. Fletcher, "The Hako: A Pawnee Ceremony," 22.

14. Fletcher, "The Hako: A Pawnee Ceremony," 22.

15. Fletcher, "The Hako: A Pawnee Ceremony," 17.

16. Dorsey, "Omaha Sociology," 205–370.

17. Fletcher, "The Omaha Tribe," 377.

18. Fletcher, "The Hako: A Pawnee Ceremony," 40.

7. CAHOKIA

1. Romain, "Monks Mound as an Axis Mundi for the Cahokian World," 27–52.

2. Pauketat, *Cahokia,* chap. 1.

3. Pauketat, *Cahokia,* chap. 3.

4. Pauketat, *Cahokia,* chap. 2.

5. Pauketat, *Cahokia,* location 328.

6. Pauketat, *Cahokia,* location 91.

7. Silverberg, *Mound Builders of Ancient America,* 26.

8. Thomas, "Report on the Mound Explorations of the Bureau of Ethnology."

9. Thomas, 700.

10. Pauketat, *Medieval Mississippians: The Cahokian World,* 14–15.

11. Pauketat, *Cahokia,* location 343.

12. Pauketat, "The Emerald Acropolis," 55–56.

13. Prentice, "An Analysis of the Symbolism Expressed by the Birger Figurine," 239–66.

14. Sharp, "Sacred Narratives of Cosmic Significance."

8. AS ABOVE, SO BELOW

1. Romain, *An Archaeology of the Sacred,* 20–24.

2. Romain, *An Archaeology of the Sacred,* 2.

3. Romain, *An Archaeology of the Sacred,* 6–10.

4. Lundy, *Sacred Geometry.*

5. Little, *The Illustrated History Encyclopedia of Native American Mounds & Earthworks.*

6. Romain, *An Archaeology of the Sacred,* 87.

7. Romain, *Mysteries of the Hopewell,* 135–142

8. Romain, *An Archaeology of the Sacred,* 49.

9. Romain, *An Archaeology of the Sacred,* 150–153.

10. Romain, *An Archaeology of the Sacred,* 156.

11. Romain, *An Archaeology of the Sacred,* 157.

12. Hamilton, xiii.

13. Fletcher and Cameron, "Serpent Mound: A Fort Ancient Icon?", 1.

14. Romain, William F., "Radiocarbon Dates Reveal Serpent Mound Is More than Two Thousand Years Old," 1–22.

15. Hardman, "The Great Serpent and the Sun," 34–40.

16. Sinclair, "The Nature of Archeoastronmy," 17.

17. Romain, "Adena-Hopewell Earthworks," 28–29.

18. Romain, "Monks Mound as an Axis Mundi for the Cahokian World," 27–52.

19. Sherrod and Rolingson, "Surveyors of the Ancient Mississippi Valley," 35.

20. Hively, "Geometry and Astronomy in Prehistoric Ohio."

21. Romain, "Adena-Hopewell Earthworks," 54–82.

22. Romain, "Adena-Hopewell Earthworks," 60.

23. Romain, "Adena-Hopewell Earthworks," 61.

24. Romain, "Adena-Hopewell Earthworks," 66.

25. Romain, "Adena-Hopewell Earthworks," 64–67.

26. Romain, "Adena-Hopewell Earthworks," 68–70.

27. Romain, "Adena-Hopewell Earthworks," 73.

9. TEN THOUSAND YEARS AGO AND BEYOND

1. Romain, "Astronomy and Geometry at Poverty Point," 42–50.

2. Romain, "Solar Alignments at the Watson Brake Site," 4.

3. Saunders, "Watson Brake," 631–668.

4. Wallis, "Introduction," 1–17.

5. Malakoff, "Rethinking Shell Middens."

6. Volusia County Historic Preservation Board and Volusia County Government, "Turtle Mound."

BIBLIOGRAPHY

Blasing, Bob. "Pawnee Animal Lodges Revisited." Paper presented at the 13th Flint Hills Conference, Lincoln, Nebraska, 1992.

Carpenter, Kristen A., and Angela R. Riley. "Standing Tall: The Sioux's battle against a Dakota oil pipeline is a galvanizing social justice movement for Native Americans." Slate, September 23, 2016.

Chandler, Kaitlyn, Wendi Field Murray, María Nieves Zedeño, Samrat Clements, and Robert James. *The Winged: An Upper Missouri River Ethno-Ornithology.* University of Arizona Press, 2016. Available at JSTOR (website).

Deloria, Vine Jr. *God Is Red.* New York: Grosset & Dunlap, 1973.

Diaz-Granados, Carol, James Richard Duncan. "Of Masks and Myths." *Midcontinental Journal of Archaeology* Vol. 25. No. 1 (Spring 2000): 1–26.

Diaz-Granados, Carol, James Richard Duncan, and F. Kent Reilly III, eds. *Picture Cave: Unraveling the Mysteries of the Mississippian Cosmos.* Austin: University of Texas Press, 2015.

Dieterle, Richard L. "The Redhorn Panel of Picture Cave: An American Star Map." Available at The Encyclopedia of Hocąk (Winnebago) Mythology (website), 2005.

Dillehay, Tom D., C. Ramirez, M. Pino, M. B. Collins, J. Rossen, and J. D. Pino-Navarro. "Monte Verde: Seaweed, Food, Medicine, and the Peopling of South America" *Science,* 320 (May 2008): 784–786.

Dorsey, Rev. J. Owen. "Omaha Sociology." In *Third Annual Report of the Bureau of Ethnology to the Secretary of the Smithsonian Institution.* Washington, D.C.: Smithsonian Institution, 1881–1882.

Dunbar-Ortiz, Roxanne. *An Indigenous Peoples' History of the United States.* Boston: Beacon Press, 2015.

Duncan, James R. "Identifying the Characters on the Walls of Picture Cave." In *Picture Cave: Unraveling the Mysteries of the Mississippian Cosmos.* Austin: University of Texas Press, 2015.

Ehler, Sidney Z., and John B. Morrall, eds, trans. *Church and State through the Centuries: A Collection of Historic Documents and Commentaries.* New York: Biblo & Tannen, 1967.

Fenton, William Nelson. *The Iroquois Eagle Dance: An Offshoot of the Calumet Dance.* Syracuse: Syracuse University Press, 1991.

Flem-Ath, Rand, and Colin Wilson. *The Atlantis Blueprint: Unlocking the Ancient Mysteries of a Long-Lost Civilization.* New York: Random House, 2000.

Fletcher, Alice C., "The Hako: A Pawnee Ceremony." In *Twenty-Second Annual Report of the Bureau of American Ethnology, Part 2.* Washington, D.C.: Smithsonian Institution, 1900–1901.

Fletcher, Alice C., and Francis La Flesche. "The Omaha Tribe." *In Twenty-Seventh Annual Report of the Bureau of American Ethnology to the Secretary of the Smithsonian Institution, 1905–1906.* Washington, D.C.: Government Printing Office, 1911.

Fletcher, Robert V., Cameron Terry L., et al. "Serpent Mound: A Fort Ancient Icon?" *Midcontinental Journal of Archaeology* 21, no. 1 (1996).

Gardner, Laurence. *The Origin of God.* London: Dash House, 2010.

Gosart, Ulia. "Who's 'Vanishing'?—Curtis' Ideas on Race and His Work." In *Performing Archive: Edward S. Curtis + "the vanishing race."* Scripps Faculty Publications and Research, 2013. Available at Scalar USC (website).

Grinnell, George Bird. "The Boy Who Was Sacrificed." In *Pawnee Hero Stories and Folk-Tales: With Notes on the Origin, Customs and Character of the Pawnee People.* University of Nebraska Press, 1961.

Hall, Robert L. *An Archaeology of the Soul: North American Indian Belief and Ritual.* University of Illinois Press, 1997.

Hamilton, Ross. *The Mystery of the Serpent Mound: In Search of the Alphabet of the Gods.* North Atlantic Books, 2000.

———. *Star Mounds: Legacy of a Native American Mystery.* North Atlantic Books, 2012.

Hardman, Clark, and Marjorie H. Hardman. "The Great Serpent and the Sun." *Ohio Archaeologist* 37, no. 3 (1987): 34–40.

Hively, Ray, and Robert Horn. "Geometry and Astronomy in Prehistoric Ohio." *Journal for the History of Astronomy* 13, no. 4 (February 1982).

Hudson, Linda S. *Mistress of Manifest Destiny: A Biography of Jane McManus Storm Cazneau, 1807–1808.* Austin, TX: Texas State Historical Association, 2001.

Johnson & Graham's Lessee v. M'Intosh. 21 U.S. (8 Wheat.) 543 (1823).

King, Cecil. Interview and conversations with Odawa elder and teacher, 2011–2012.

Lepper, Bradley T. *Ohio Archaeology: An Illustrated Chronicle of Ohio's Ancient American Indian Cultures.* Wilmington, OH: Orange Frazer Press, 2005.

Malakoff, David. "Rethinking Shell Middens." *American Archaeology* 22, no. 2 (Summer 2018).

Menzies, Gavin. *The Lost Empire of Atlantis: History's Greatest Mystery Revealed.* Swordfish / Orion Publishing Group, 2011.

Merk, Frederick, and Lois Bannister Merk. *Manifest Destiny and Mission in American History: A Reinterpretation.* New York: Vintage Books, 1963.

Mufson, Steven, and Juliet Eilperin. "Trump seeks to revive Dakota Access, Keystone SL oil pipelines." *Washington Post,* January 24, 2017.

Murie, James R., and Douglas R. Parks. "Ceremonies of the Pawnee." *Smithsonian Contributions to Anthropology* 27 (1981).

Nabokov, Peter. *Where the Lightning Strikes: The Lives of American Indian Sacred Places.* London: Penguin Books, 2007.

Napolskikh, Vladimir. "The Earth-Diver Myth (A812) in Northern Eurasia and North America: Twenty Years Later." In *Mythic Discourses: Studies in Uralic Traditions,* edited by Anna-Leena Siikala Frog and Eila Stepanova, 120–140. Finnish Literature Society, 2012.

Newell, Margaret Ellen. *Brethren by Nature: New England Indians, Colonists, and the Origins of American Slavery.* Ithaca: Cornell University Press, 2016.

Page, Jake. *In the Hands of the Great Spirit: The 20,000 Year History of American Indians.* New York: Free, 2004.

Parks, Douglas R., and Waldo R. Wedel. "Pawnee Geography: Historical and Sacred." *Great Plains Quarterly* 5, no. 3 (Summer 1985).

Pauketat, Timothy R. *Cahokia: Ancient America's Great City on the Mississippi.* New York: Viking Penguin, 2009.

Pauketat, Timothy R. and Susan M. Alt. *Medieval Mississippians: The Cahokian World.* Santa Fe, NM: SAR Press, 2015.

Pauketat, Timothy R., Susan M. Alt, and Jeffery D. Kruchten. "The Emerald Acropolis: Elevating the Moon and Water in the Rise of Cahokia." *Antiquity* 91, no. 355 (2017): 207–22.

Pope Alexander VI, *Inter Caetera* by Pope Alexander VI. 1493.

Porter, J. R. *The Lost Bible: Forgotten Scriptures Revealed*. Chicago: University of Chicago Press, 2001.

Powell, John Wesley. "On Limitations To The Use of Some Anthropological Data." In *First Annual Report of the Bureau of American Ethnology to the Secretary of the Smithsonian Institution 1879–1880*. Washington, D.C.: Government Printing Office, 1881.

Prentice, Guy. "An Analysis of the Symbolism Expressed by the Birger Figurine." *American Antiquity* 51, no. 02 (April 1986).

Red Corn, Kathryn. "The Spider in the Cave." In *Picture Cave: Unraveling the Mysteries of the Mississippian Cosmos*. Austin: University of Texas Press, 2015.

Romain, William F. *An Archaeology of the Sacred: Adena-Hopewell Astronomy and Landscape Archaeology*. The Ancient Earthworks Project, 2015.

———. "Adena-Hopewell Earthworks and the Milky Way Path of Souls." In *Tracing the Relational: The Archaeology of Worlds, Spirits, and Temporalities*, edited by Meghan E. Buchanan and B. Jacob Skousen. Salt Lake City: University of Utah Press, 2015.

———. "Monks Mound as an Axis Mundi for the Cahokian World." *Illinois Archaeology* 29 (2017).

———. *Mysteries of the Hopewell: Astronomers, Geometers, and Magicians of the Eastern Woodlands*. Akron, OH: University of Akron Press, 2000.

———. "Newark Earthwork Cosmology: This Island Earth." *The Newsletter of Hopewell Archeology in the Ohio River Valley* 6, no. 2 (March 2005): 2–5.

Romain, William F., and Norman L. Davis. "Solar Alignments at the Watson Brake Site." *Louisiana Archaeology* 36 (2007, 2012).

———. "Astronomy and Geometry at Poverty Point." *Louisiana Archaeology*, no. 38 (2011).

Romain, William F., Edward W. Hermann, G. William Monaghan, and Jarrod Burks. "Radiocarbon Dates Reveal Serpent Mound Is More Than Two Thousand Years Old." *Midcontinental Journal of Archaeology* 42, no. 3 (2017): 201–22.

Sandoz, Mari. *Love Song to the Plains*. New York: Harper & Brothers, 1961.

Saunders, J., R. Mandel, C. Sampson, C. Allen, E. Allen, D. Bush, J. K. Feathers,

K. J. Gremillion, C. T. Hallmark, and H. E. Jackson, et al. "Watson Brake, a Middle Archaic Mound Complex in Northeast Louisiana." *American Antiquity* 70, no. 4 (2005): 631–68.

Sharp, Robert. "Sacred Narratives of Cosmic Significance: The Place of the Keesee Figurine in the Mississippian Mythos." In *Visions of Other Worlds: Ideological and Ritual Functions of Mississippian Symbols,* edited by Kevin E. Smith. Gainesville: University Press of Florida, 2014.

Sherrod, Clay P., and Martha Ann Rolingson. "Surveyors of the Ancient Mississippi Valley." *Arkansas Archaeological Survey Research Series,* no. 28 (1987).

Silverberg, Robert. *Mound Builders of Ancient America: The Archaeology of a Myth.* Greenwich, CT: New York Graphic Society, 1968.

Sinclair, R. M. "The Nature of Archaeoastronomy." In *Viewing the Sky Through Past and Present Cultures: Selected Papers from the Oxford VII International Conference on Archaeoastronomy,* edited by Todd W. Bostwick and Bryan Bates. Phoenix: City of Phoenix Parks Recreation and Library, 2006.

Spence, Lewis. *The History of Atlantis.* Dover, 2003. First published 1926 by Rider & Son, Ltd. (London and New York).

Starita, Joe. *"I Am a Man": Chief Standing Bear's Journey for Justice.* New York: St. Martin's Press, 2008.

"Steeling for a Fight: Donald Trump Backs Two Big Oil Pipelines." *The Economist,* January 28, 2017.

Stoecker, William B. "The Dragon Factor: Why Do Some Believe the Myths Could Be Truer Than We Thought?" *Atlantis Rising,* no. 119 (September/ October 2016).

Teuton, Christopher B. *Stories of the Turtle Island Liars Club.* Chapel Hill, NC: University of North Carolina Press, 2012.

Thomas, Cyrus. "Report on the Mound Explorations of the Bureau of Ethnology." In *Twelfth Annual Report of the Bureau of American Ethnology to the Secretary of the Smithsonian Institution 1890–1891.* Washington, D.C.: Government Printing Office, 1894.

Volusia County Historic Preservation Board and Volusia County Government. "Turtle Mound Located in the Canaveral National Seashore."

Waldman, Carl. *Atlas of the North American Indian.* New York: Checkmark Books, 2009.

Wallis, Neill J., and Asa R. Randall, eds. "Introduction." In *New Histories of Pre-Columbian Florida.* Gainesville, FL: University Press of Florida, 2014.

Wegener, Alfred. *The Origin of the Continents and Oceans.* Translated by John Biram. New York: Dover, 1966. First published in Germany, 1915.

Wishart, David J. *An Unspeakable Sadness: The Dispossession of the Nebraska Indians.* Lincoln, NE.: University of Nebraska Press, 1997.

Worster, Donald. *A River Running West: The Life of John Wesley Powell.* Oxford: Oxford University Press, 2001.

INDEX